1

*A*nne Blake looked around the bright bedroom from the edge of the blanket. She squinted as she peeked, so surprised when the cold, dark walls of the cottage did not greet her. Smooth satin brushed her cheek as she pushed back the bedding to view more. The lace curtains cast patterns of shadow and light on the carpet beside her bed. The brightness originated from the back window which must face the east she surmised.

When the maid led her upstairs the afternoon before, she had assumed they headed to the mistress' room. When her trunk arrived, and the maid asked if she wished help with unpacking, she understood the room was hers. The thought of it still caused her disbelief.

Anne moved her gaze around the room. Along the longest wall, a small writing desk and chair waited by the bright windows. Further along that same wall was a wash stand with a basin and pitcher below an oval mirror in a gold frame. The wash stand stood next to the hallway door. Her bed against the wall on the other side had small tables on each side. Next to the one on the right was the dresser where she had spread her few garments thinly through three of the five drawers. The last corner held a mirror in a stand that allowed it to swivel. The pale-yellow walls were decorated with paintings of rose bouquets. The furnishings, though spare, were far more than had ever been hers to enjoy.

Faint sounds from the kitchen signaled the beginning of a new day. Her arrival the day before to the home of the famous artist, Mary Moser, had been fraught with such anxiety that she had not been able to eat. This morning, she found she was quite hungry. She swung her legs around and out of the covers. No cold flagstones met her feet. Instead, they landed on a soft wool carpet. She tidied the bedding with some pride of keeping her room as she first observed it. She found it difficult to grasp that it would be she who returned to sleep in such luxury again that night.

Anne dressed to proceed downstairs. She wore one of her three dark wool dresses that had been her uniforms when she worked for the family of the Duke, months ago. She had taken good care of the clothes, stretching their use by mending and hemming as necessary. She owned two other gowns, but they were inappropriate for day wear, having used them when escorting the Duke's children downstairs. So much had come to pass since then, but she would not trouble her mind with thoughts of Lord Greville and the household she had left yesterday. Doing so would only expose the fresh wounds on her heart left by a man she would never see again. She had new worries and new emotions with which to contend.

As she entered the kitchen, a maid jumped from her stool as if frightened by the sight of her.

"Oh, I am so sorry, Miss. I did not know you were awake. If you had but rung the bell-", she said, bowing in contrition.

MISS *Moser's Student*

"I did not wish to disturb you." Anne did not explain that she had never pulled a cord to summon a maid in her life. She did not discuss it further as she was not sure of her position in the household. Anne was not one to put on airs, but she had experienced trouble at Lord Greville's manor with one jealous maid, and she hoped to begin anew here at Miss Moser's home.

"If you take a seat, I will serve you some breakfast. Would you like tea? Mrs. Holgate will boil an egg or two if you would like, and there are fresh, sweet buns."

There were several stools along the counter and Anne pulled up the one next to where the maid had been seated. Before she could sit, the maid spoke up. "Oh no, Miss. I will serve you in the dining room." She indicated the room next door. "Miss Moser has taken her breakfast in her room and asks that you visit her when you have finished."

Anne was reluctant to put forth her order. She did not wish to inconvenience the maid any more than she obviously was doing. The maid had shown no sign of disapproval as she had waited for Anne to indicate what she wished to eat.

"Tea would be nice, and eggs sound wonderful. I find I am hungry this morning," Anne said, as she took her place in the other room as instructed. The kitchen maids had been quite kind to her the night before urging her to eat when she had little appetite. They offered substitutions thinking she disliked what was offered. Finally, Miss Moser had waved them all away, and the two had conversed about Anne's past and how she had come to live at Lord Greville's manor.

Anne told a short version of her life previous to the time she spent at Lord Greville's estate. She gave an explanation about the incident with the Duke's nephew, the cause of her dismissal. She could tell Miss Moser did not judge her for what had come to pass. On the subject of Lord Greville, Anne could hardly speak, except to say she had come to live with her father, the lord's head gardener.

"Sir Joseph Banks told the story of a maid burning the fine drawings you made of Lord Greville's flowering plants. He spoke of your successful completion of over fifty paintings for the lord. How distressing that must have been for you."

It was obvious she knew nothing of Anne's trespass into the lord's library, and how she had come to serve Lord Greville in making the drawings as a punishment. She did not tell the story of how the lord had found a drawing in his library that fateful day. The drawing had given her away. It was that same drawing that he had kept to himself that enticed Miss Moser to take her on as a student. It warmed her heart that Lord Greville had spoken of her to Sir Joseph Banks.

"I did not think of the drawings as mine, but a record of his lordship's plants. For him, I felt quite sorry." Anne dared not say more as she could feel her chin start to quiver and her lips begin to pout. She did not want to reveal her distress to her new employer.

Miss Moser sensed Anne's anguish. Admiring her features, she saw that the young woman sitting across from her could be very pretty. The girl had a tired, somber look, as if she had been underfed and sickly for months, though Miss Moser did not believe Anne had been mistreated. The mass of brown curls that spilled off her shoulders framed her equally dark eyes, small nose, and delicate mouth. Her eyes showed an intensity that was masked by a brooding sadness the elderly woman saw within them. Miss Moser supposed the death of her father might account for the girl's wan face. Her heart went out to her new student.

"We will begin tomorrow with some basics. I have several exercises I customarily have my students complete. The lessons give a general knowledge of color, shading, and perspective. Then we will continue onto the care of brushes, some facts about mixing paint, and specifically the layering of paint on the canvas. I am aware you have never work with oils," the teacher continued, referring to the use of oil paints. "So, we have much to do to get you started. You will continue with water colors, but I think you will enjoy the freedom that oils provide. Once you are painting, we will study the symmetry of objects, direction of light, and the use of color to indicate dimension within a work."

Anne could not understand how she should warrant such attention. "I did not expect such instruction. I am very much excited to become a better artist, but I also wish to serve you in any way I can to repay you for this opportunity."

"If you are the good student that I believe you will be, that will be my benefit. I trust Lord Greville would not have sought this arrangement if he had not held complete confidence in your ability to advance. I look forward to our time together." They had ended their conversation at that point and each retired to their bedrooms for the night. Anne had no more put her head to her pillow and pulled the soft coverlet up around her neck before sleep took all her concerns away.

With her breakfast finished, Anne was ready to start the first day of instruction. She looked forward to seeking out the elderly artist who had shown her nothing but kindness. As she set her napkin by her plate, Anne heard voices coming from the back entrance and the servant's hall. One voice belonged to the head housekeeper, Mrs. Marshall. Another voice of a man, low and gravelly, spoke very quickly, explaining something to the housekeeper. As they came closer, Anne could distinguish the man's words.

Mrs. Marshall entered the kitchen pressed on by the man. Anne noted the difference between this housekeeper and Mrs. Lambert, Lord Greville's head housekeeper. Mrs. Lambert wielded her power in an unconditional way, but this woman seemed to be unable to stop the forward progress of the man with the husky voice.

"We usually walk through the rooms and see which ones could use a bit of cheering up, with paint, you know. Then we gives you a price and starts painting, as soon as we can fit you in," he was saying. The man was of a large build and he towered over the small housekeeper. The maids had moved to the other end of the kitchen, away from the burly man.

"But we have a man who does painting and such," Mrs. Marshall was trying to argue back, but the much larger man kept coming, almost pushing the housekeeper out of the way. As Mrs. Marshall realized she was losing control, she called out for help.

"Hodges!" she yelled.

The would-be painter was now standing in the kitchen facing the dining area where Anne was sitting. He made his way across the room and was just about to approach her when Hodges came in from the front hall. In three long strides, the butler came to stand directly in front of the man impeding any further progress toward Anne. The painter wore a wide brimmed brown hat and a loose coat of the same color tied with a leather belt. Though these appeared to be his work clothes, there was no evidence of paint on them. He stopped in his tracks when he saw Hodges coming. The tall butler, who had to duck many of the door frames, also weighed in heavily with a lean, but muscular frame. He presented a formidable foe to the painter.

"Sorry, sir, but I was going to take a look at the rooms and determine where I should start with the painting." He tipped his brown hat and then thought to remove it, revealing a ring of straw-like hair forming a nest around a balding head. He backed to the corner of the dining room against the window as if to take in a view of the room in its entirety.

"See there, in the corner, that needs new paint," the man said.

Anne and Mrs. Marshall looked up at the corner and Hodges only glanced. Anne thought what the man pointed out was only a shadow.

"Ah, but we did not call for a painter," the butler said.

Anne wondered at Hodges' composure and the polite manner with which he spoke to the man. It seemed uncommon for him to address a lower-stationed man with such gallantry, but it was not Anne's business.

Hodges escorted the painter back out of the dining room and through the kitchen asking him his name and how he might contact him when they did have need of a painter.

The man seemed to pause, looking at his partner who had waited at the kitchen door.

"Uh, Muggins," he said, "Sam Muggins."

"And how should I find you, Mr. Muggins?" the butler inquired.

"Just ask around at Jackson's. They'll know where to find me." With that and Hodges' strong arm across the man's back, the painter and his partner departed.

Mrs. Marshall looked at Hodges, shaking her head and regaining her composure.

Hodges returned to the dining room and came to Anne. "I trust you slept well, Miss? Sorry for the disturbance."

"Yes, very well. You were quite kind to the man," Anne said, wondering, but not asking directly.

"Yes, well, I do not believe he is a painter. I fear he is a thief. We must be careful with his type. He came to peruse a way in and out and what he would take with him. He is to be pitied, to have chosen such a vocation."

Anne listened to Hodges and felt he spoke as if he were a member of the clergy, rather than the mistress' butler. She felt privileged to be included in his circle as one of the household.

Hodges had been able to size up the young lady rather quickly. Her humble mannerisms and intelligent conversation impressed him. He took a liking to the girl almost at once. He felt she might make an excellent companion for Miss Moser and important addition as the lady's eyesight continued to diminish.

As Anne began to push her chair back to leave the dining table, Hodges quickly came to pull it out for her.

"I am afraid we are not accustomed to anyone but the mistress taking meals," he said.

"Oh, I hope I will not add to anyone's duties. I am quite capable of caring for myself, and not at all accustomed to being waited upon," Anne answered honestly. She did not want the staff of the household to hold any grudge against her good fortune. Hodges gave a warm smile that Anne met with one of her own, happy to have formed a friendship so quickly. She turned to head up the stairs.

The maid showed Anne to Miss Moser's room and knocked softly. With the words "come in", she opened the door and let Anne pass through. Much like the studio room where Anne had first been received by the artist, this room was also cheerful and feminine. Shades were drawn halfway down the windows creating a soft cast of morning light on the room. The walls were papered in pink with chains of magenta rose buds forming stripes. The bed was covered with a dark pink satin cover, and all around the room were lovely pieces of furniture, white with gold trim. The only item that was neither white nor pink was the brown Siamese cat curled up next to Miss Moser on the bed.

The elderly lady sat against a pile of pillows with a small tray on her lap. She wore a pink bed jacket. A white bonnet was tied loosely around her head. She had a pile of letters and a magnifier on the tray with a cup, saucer, and an empty plate which she now slid off her lap as Anne entered. The cat also stood and stretched as the young woman came toward the bed, examining the new guest.

"Sit here, dear," Miss Moser requested. She pointed to the delicate chair beside the end of her bed. Anne studied the lady's smile; it stretched from one ruddy cheek to the other. Miss Moser did not have the angular features of the nobility for whom Anne had served in her past. She did not act arrogant in the way Anne had noticed noble men and women usually addressed those of

Anne's order. The elderly artist looked more like a farmer's wife and had the easy mannerisms of such. Anne was immediately comfortable in her presence.

As soon as Anne sat down, the cat jumped from the bed onto her lap. Anne had never been so close to a cat before and held her arms up awkwardly. The cat sniffed the air and then settled on her lap in a tight circle with his tail wrapped around the outside.

"Oh, Edward, what are you doing to poor Miss Blake? He does not usually take to strangers so readily, but he seems completely besotted. He will not bite or scratch. If he had avoided you, I might have been more worried about his behavior. Once he has made a friend, it is forever, and he has chosen you quite quickly. How delightful. Is it a bother?"

"No, Ma'am, I am just not much acquainted with cats, but it is no trouble if he wants to sit here." Anne let her arms down along her lap, and the cat rested against them purring.

The two women chatted about nothing important for several minutes. Miss Moser asked about Anne's room and was assured by the young woman that she was delighted with her new accommodations. They spoke briefly of the painter's odd visit, and then onto the weather. Miss Moser commented that she wished it might snow one day soon as it had been a drier winter than usual so far. The elderly artist also listed some upcoming events. Anne tried to be attentive, but so much of what the lady said seemed foreign. She understood only bits of what she mentioned. Anne doubted she would have any part in the lady's plans, but still she thought she should show interest even if she did not follow the conversation.

"I find that my eyes are very sore this morning. I stayed too long in the sun yesterday. I will not go to the studio until the afternoon, but if you would like to start on a sketch until we are together, I believe you saw where the paper is kept and pencils are in a container on the desk." Miss Moser attempted to wiggle away from her breakfast tray. Anne began to rise to remove the tray, forgetting she was held down by a cat. Her movement stirred the cat that jumped down to enjoy a slice of sunshine on the floor.

"Oh do not trouble with the tray. Millie will return in a moment," the elderly lady said.

"It is no trouble, Mistress," Anne replied, taking up the tray from the lady's lap.

Miss Moser looked at Anne and saw a look in her eyes that caused her to ask, "What is it, dear? What are you thinking?"

Anne stood holding the tray, remembering what she was thinking and without fore thought answered the elderly woman honestly, "So much has come to pass to cause me to be here. I do not wish to be a burden to you in any way. It is not beneath me to help with your breakfast tray, or any of the maid's duties to which you might wish me to tend. I spent too many idle hours at Lord Greville's manor, and I do not wish to do so here. Above all, I wish to have some purpose to my life. I so appreciate what Lord Greville provided by sending me to you."

"Oh, nonsense. You come well recommended by two sponsors who feel you are meant to be here."

"Two sponsors?" Anne asked.

"Yes. Lord Greville and Sir Joseph Banks."

"I have never met Sir Joseph Banks. How can he champion me?" Anne asked.

"I believe he has seen your work and recognizes your skills, and the need for further training. These two drawings, for instance, perhaps others?"

Once again, Anne's heart skipped a beat. It was such a surprise to find her lost drawings in Miss Moser's possession. Lord Greville had kept them for all that time, and she had never known.

"No, there are no others," Anne clarified. She had burnt all her earlier sketches in the days following Lord Greville's departure to

Wales. She had believed she would never draw again, burying her art supplies deep into her trunk. That seemed a lifetime ago, and yet it was only months.

Miss Moser took up the paintings sitting on her bedside table and held them out to Anne. "You may want to finish these. I see quite a difference between the two pictures and how much you improved while painting for Lord Greville."

Anne had seen how daily practice and a little instruction from the book Lord Greville presented to her had certainly improved her skills, though it had all come to naught when the maid, Becky, burned her drawings in a fit of rage. Only the two drawings Lord Greville had saved remained of her time at Paddington. Her heart ached and tears came into her eyes.

Miss Moser saw the girl's expression change. "You have much regard for Lord Greville," she said.

"I do not think of anyone more highly than I do Lord Greville. I hope I am worthy of his decision to send me here." In her mind, she thought of her last days at the lord's manor and how much she longed to remain. Her only hope for her future had been to stay with him. She had not imagined being sent to the aging artist or what benefits might come her way.

"Surely you are worthy, Miss Blake, Anne. Someday we will show Lord Greville so. I will join you in the studio soon." She indicated the conversation's end.

Anne's heartache eased to hear such a statement. The thought of seeing Lord Greville again lifted her heart, and a smile returned to her face. Mary Moser noticed the change. She wondered how Lord Greville felt about the girl. Her curiosity would prod her to look into the matter. Anne took the tray and bowed as she headed out the pink room's door with a light step and a cheerful smile.

2

A nne decided to sketch the honeysuckle vines as represented on Miss Moser's studio wallpaper. She added a fence for the vine to trail upon, thinking of the view along the back edge of Lord Greville's kitchen garden. She worked on the drawing while sitting in the front window, daydreaming. Mostly, she was watching passersby on the street below. She had never witnessed such a busy scene, having never lived in the city. At noon, a maid came to fetch her for a midday meal.

Upon her return from the meal, Miss Moser arrived, followed by a maid who carried an orange on a plate. Anne turned her attention to the elderly lady who placed the orange in the middle of a sheet of paper on her desk. The light from the window cast a shadow behind the orange as Miss Moser moved the fruit around, seeking the best placement.

"There, that will do for a while. We may have to move it as you are working to retain the same angle of the sun." Miss Moser looked up to make sure she had Anne's attention. "I wish for you to draw the orange and its shadow to the best of your ability. You can see that it is almost black where the orange meets the paper, and then turns to the lightest of grays by the edge. The edge of the orange is without color or detail where the light is the strongest. This is an exercise for pencil only as I wish for you to understand shading and how the light affects the view."

Anne found the pencils in a cup on the desk, but Miss Moser chose one for her before she could make a choice. "I believe a softer lead will make the exercise easier for you. Start softly, and increase the pressure as you increase the darkness."

Miss Moser left the room and did not return for half an hour. In that time, Anne had finished the shape of the orange and had begun forming the outer edge of the shadow. Upon the artist's return, Miss Moser turned the paper under the orange to the same angle as before. She took a quick look at how far Anne had come with her rendering, pleasantly surprised at how well the girl was progressing.

Anne continued on as Miss Moser examined two notes brought to her by Millie. Anne noticed she smiled as she read one of them. Anne twisted the square pencil in her hand in order to find the sharp point. She worked on the darkest part of the shadow underneath the fruit.

When Miss Moser looked up, she saw Anne had stopped drawing and wondered if the young artist was finished. Looking across her desk to Anne, she saw that indeed she had completed the exercise to the utmost degree of success and with such ease. Miss Moser realized her new student had a keen eye that she might be a pleasure to instruct rather than a duty.

"That is excellent, my dear. Please sign and date your exercise in the bottom right corner. We will begin a portfolio for you. I have a set of boards tied together leaning against the side of my desk for you to use. Now, let us step into the parlor across the hall as it is teatime."

Anne was surprised that it was so late into the afternoon. She had concentrated on shading the orange so intently that time slipped by unnoticed. She was glad to lift her eyes and felt her stomach growl for lack of food. She crossed the hall through wide double doors to the room that adjoined the pink bedroom.

A cup of tea and a sandwich restored Anne and gave her a chance to ask a few more questions of her new mistress. She did not ask the question she wished an answer to more than any other, knowing it would be unseemly. To ask if she had heard anything more from Lord Greville when they had spoken of the man the day before would certainly draw attention to her thoughts. Instead, she asked the elderly artist about the Royal Academy.

"My father was the first president, and he had much influence over the decisions there for many years. In fact, it is probably the only reason I was inducted as a member as well as my dear friend, Angelica Kaufmann. She might have been allowed by her merits as a most accomplished historical painter, but my flowers might have come with some objections from many members if not for my father's control and the friendship of several of the other artists." Miss Moser smiled in a way that let Anne know she did not hold any animosity against her fellows.

"Just this afternoon, I have received a note from a member, still hounding me to take up the presidency. I have no desire to do so, and yet I am honored several of the members nominated me for the position for last year's election. I find I go to fewer and fewer of the meetings though I am still involved with the annual show and the awarding of medals. Perhaps, we can attend a meeting at some point. A visit to the academy will open your eyes to the possibilities for improvement that such an institution can offer, not only to men, but women also."

Anne thought timidly of such an outing. She had heard of the lady's involvement with the school, but to accompany her in the presence of such famous artists was inconceivable.

When their tea time was finished, Anne rose to go to her room not knowing that Miss Moser studied her as she was leaving. The elbows of the young girl's dark blue dress were worn thin; the weave was showing. The pink of her skin was evident. The hem of the dress was shorter by inches than when it was new as it had been stitched up several times showing a bit of her ankle. The collar at the sides of the young woman's neck was beginning to fray.

"Anne," Miss Moser called.

Anne turned to face the lady.

"I wonder if you have any dresses that are not of this dark color?"

Anne thought for a moment, but surely her other two dresses were not appropriate for daily use. They had once been walking dresses belonging to the Duke's daughters.

"No, Ma'am. These dresses were made for my service with the Duke. I have used them since that time. I only have the three, all dark."

"My dress maker comes on Thursday. I would like her to fit you for three new dresses, Anne. I do not like to see you in such drab apparel. It does not suit my mood or your spirit."

Anne was taken aback by the lady's desires, and it showed on her face.

"I hope you will allow me this," Miss Moser added, to soften the blow her comments seemed to have caused the young woman.

There was no room for argument against the way the subject was introduced, though Anne worried at the lady's expense.

"I would love a new dress," Anne said humbly. "I did not expect you to go to such expense on my behalf. I feel I have done nothing to deserve it. That is all."

"Ah, did I not say you had two good sponsors?" The lady answered quickly with a wink and a smile.

Anne puzzled at the remark, but thanked her mentor again and left the room quickly. She trotted to her room and shut the door behind her, shaking with anger. Had Lord Greville paid Miss Moser to take her? Is that what the lady implied? Had the kiss she had shared with the nobleman resulted in a necessary resolution? Did money play a part in her being sent away days later?

In the last two days, Anne had settled into her new home feeling the comforts of Miss Moser's care. The unexpected kindness shown by everyone in the household and the wonderful opportunity she had been given were enjoyed with utmost pleasure. Miss Moser had even mentioned Lord Greville a time or two which gave Anne a feeling they were still connected.

Now with the lady's comments, that bliss was swept away as Anne realized she did not come to be here by any merit of her own, but as a solution to the lord's big problem, her. There were frightening similarities between being caught with the Duke's nephew in a compromised position and the kiss with Lord Greville. In both cases she had taken the blame, been sent away, and was forced to make a change for these men's errors. The fact could not have hit Anne harder than if she had been beaten. It appeared she was some sort of commodity that these people took in when it was convenient and passed on without a care or concern when not.

Once again she had tried to fool herself into believing she had been something special to someone, trusting them with her heart. Instead, she had been cast off as unneeded. She had been sent to this new mistress with a dowry to ensure she did not return.

Tears did not come. She was livid. Then and there she vowed not to allow such a mistake again. She was alone in this world. Her heart closed a door that she had always kept wide open. No one would know the change, but from this moment on, Anne would never put herself in a position where anyone could hurt her so easily again.

She stretched across her bed wishing she could cry, but the ache in her stomach did not lead to tears. Instead, a knot of determination formed deep inside. She was resolved to show them all and rise above these past injustices. Miss Moser would find that Anne meant to succeed.

When dinner was ready, Anne did not want to face Miss Moser, but had no good excuse to explain an absence. She forced her feet down the stairs at the call for dinner. She positioned the best smile she could across her lips as she entered the room where the elderly artist sat waiting in the candlelight.

"I hope you are hungry, dear," Miss Moser said.

She was not, but replied politely, "Yes, some."

Miss Moser heard a crack in Anne's voice and wondered if the girl was somewhat homesick. After all, she was quite young, her father had died, and she had been removed from her duties at Paddington so suddenly.

"Would you care for a little wine?" she asked, thinking a bit of wine might soothe the girl's nerves.

"I have never tasted wine," Anne answered, a little surprised at the offer. Wine was an expensive commodity, Anne knew, and not to be wasted on one who might have no appreciation. Yet, she did wish to try some as in the past she had never been allowed. "I would like to try just a little."

Miss Moser made a gesture to the footman standing behind her. He immediately poured Anne a glass of beautiful plum-colored liquid that glowed in the light of the candles' flames. Anne took the glass in her hand and began to raise it as she looked to the mistress who displayed the correct grip on the glass' stem. She used her finger tips in a dainty feminine poise as she lifted the glass to her mouth and took just a sip. Anne mimicked the lady and found the initial flavor bitter. In only a moment though, the liquid spread across her tongue with a delightful essence of the outdoors, woodsy and fresh. Anne took another larger sip before putting the glass down, letting the fruity, yet acid taste linger in her throat before swallowing.

When she looked up, Miss Moser was smiling at her. Anne was reminded of the first time she tasted candied ginger and how warm Lord Greville's smile had been as he watched her make faces. Anne pulled in her thoughts, not allowing her anger of the afternoon to return. The wine was having an effect. Determined not to care so much about Lord Greville, it was Miss Moser to whom she now directed her thoughts.

"Do you like the wine?" the lady asked.

"Yes, it is sour first, but then sweet. I feel a little tingle. Perhaps I am drunk."

Miss Moser snickered, and took up her napkin to hide her sound. "If you are drunk after two sips, I will not be able to let you have more," she teased.

"I suppose I do not know. I do feel more at ease." With that new feeling, Anne spoke to the realization she had turned over in her mind all afternoon. "I am thankful for all that you have shown me this afternoon, but if you would rather not teach me, I will be happy to serve you in other capacities."

It was a sad statement. Miss Moser wondered at its source. The girl was so somber.

"My dear, it will be a delight to teach you. You have no idea of the difficult students I have worked with in the past. Queen Charlotte's daughters, the princesses, had no real ability for art. Only Princess Elizabeth showed a propensity for drawing by copying. She enjoyed the craft as none of her sisters did, trying a variety of mediums while all the while copying the work of others. Lovely girls as they were, they tried to improve as was proper. Their mother so hoped for an artist, but there was no true ability. I suffered for their lack and made as good a lesson plan as was possible. In fact, they never could shade the orange correctly. After only a few months, I suggested they should concentrate on other endeavors. Finally, their mother agreed."

Anne was amazed. The elderly woman was not only speaking of the royal family, but criticizing them.

Miss Moser continued, "Margaret Meen continued to work with Princess Elizabeth and was able to teach the girl enough to impress her poor mother. The Princess and I painted murals of flowers and birds at the Queen's residence at Frogmoor. Her mother was very pleased and proud. I enjoyed the lively company, but in general, those girls were so sheltered they could barely move about the castle grounds. I was never allowed to take them outside the walls to paint."

Still, Anne wished the mistress to understand she knew now the lessons had come at a cost to Lord Greville. Anne felt she should relieve the elderly lady from her end of the exchange. She did not wish to trouble anyone further, so she restated her resolve.

"I have been thinking that the arrangement between you and my kind sponsors need not include your attention. I am willing to be of service without your efforts."

Again, Miss Moser heard the sad regard with which the girl took in her world, as if she were wholly unworthy.

"Don't be silly. I will hear no more of this sort of talk. You are a gifted artist. I am only going to teach you how to make better use of your talent. No more of it, do you hear?" Miss Moser said firmly, but with a soft smile indicating she was not angry.

Anne was reminded once again of Lord Greville and his speech concerning his mistress, Emma Hamilton. He had said almost those same words to Anne when she had asked if he had sent Emma off to settle his debts as everyone gossiped. He had replied that Emma was like a gem he had found that needed polishing to expose her beauty. Anne quelled her anger with another sip of wine before beginning on her bowl of soup. Her heart was still distressed, but her appetite had returned.

3

The entire household was in bed and asleep by nine. Anne felt so tired when she climbed into the soft linens. Emotional turmoil was wearing. She quelled the heartache of wishing for her past by thinking about all that was new. They were all, everyone, kind to her and accepting. Though she longed for her father and the members of the household at Lord Greville's estate, she tried not to think of the lord himself. She still had not reckoned with being sent away.

Anne was sure she was tired enough to drop right off to sleep, but her mind turned every event of the day over one more time. She kept thinking about how she had been so fortunate to become Miss Moser's student, though that led in a circle back to Lord Greville and her time at Paddington. She would think of it no more. She would not pine for what was lost. She rolled over on her side one last time, resolved to let her mind rest. She had only to scoot under these wonderful blankets to know whatever happened next would be alright.

The fire broke out sometime in the early morning hours. By the time the police came to Miss Moser's door, pounding and shouting to awaken the household, the servants were already astir. Anne crept from her bed to listen at her door. She heard the word "fire". She ran back in her room to the corner window. An eerie orange glow reflected in the flickering haze and smoke. She watched for several minutes before climbing back into her bed to get warm.

Only a few minutes later, there was a knock on her door. Opening it to a wide-eyed maid, Anne could smell the smoke coming up the staircase from the front door.

"Excuse me, Miss. I do not wish to frighten you, but the constable has asked that we be prepared to leave if the need arise though he felt we were not in immediate danger. Hodges has asked that you pack a small selection of clothes and things you hold dear in the event we must make an exit."

"I would be glad to aid with any packing should it be needed," Anne called to the maid who hurried off as if she did not hear. It felt so odd to not give a hand in such a situation.

Anne shut her door to keep the thin layer of smoke from entering from the hall, even as she smelled it seeping in through her windows on that side. She looked about her room. She had nothing of value other than her few art supplies, a tin of candied ginger, a book of drawing instruction, and a pair of the lovely white gloves; all gifts from Lord Greville. She would pack her mother and father's silhouettes and her father's pipe and sweater.

Before Anne could return to her bed, there was another knock at the door. When Anne opened it, the mousey maid, Millie, was waiting. Millie was the upstairs maid. Although she seemed to be Mistress Moser's maid, there were no qualms about her bringing Anne water for her basin or turning down Anne's bed.

"Mistress says she'd like to see you, if you are awake."

"Yes, of course," Anne replied, and followed the girl through Miss Moser's door.

"Oh, Anne!" The elderly woman said with some concern. "I pity my neighbors. Such a loss. Hodges believes the firemen have got the fire in the structure under control with no further houses to be affected. He said there was no loss of life. I hope he is right." Miss Moser was standing by a box on a stand. She had a silk purse in her hand and moved other smaller bags to the purse. Anne realized that she was sorting some of her jewelry perhaps in case they found it necessary to evacuate for the fire.

"Are you alright, dear?" she asked.

"Yes, I have been watching the glow from my window, and it does appear to be lessening. It must be so sad to lose all one's belongings in such a catastrophe." Anne could only imagine if Miss Moser's house caught on fire. Looking about the room, she saw so many beautiful things that would be lost.

"I think I will have an early cup of tea, would you like to join me?" Anne began to say no as she thought of their conversation the day before, still unsure of the arrangement with Lord Greville. Her ire was quick to rise. Then she reminded herself that it was not this kind lady with whom she was angry. Miss Moser's voice held a certain appeal. Perhaps she was more frightened than she let on. It would be the right thing to stay with her awhile as a comfort. The fire was close even if under control.

"Yes, I will stay," Anne replied, dousing her angry reluctance with the woman's kindheartedness. Whatever Lord Greville had intended, mostly to be rid of her, she had found nothing but good people in this household.

So, their day began before daylight. The noise outside increased as traffic from wagons, firemen, neighbors and gawkers filled up the street. Miss Moser's household was favored by a wind that blew the smoke in the opposite direction. By afternoon the traffic thinned out and several police stood about answering questions and keeping the curious public back from the smoldering structure, now dangerous in its instability. As evening came on, the smoke settled over the entire neighborhood and the acrid smell permeated Miss Moser's home. By nightfall, the household quieted as everyone had been awakened at such an early hour. By the time the lamps along the street were lit, most of the house was dark.

Anne fell asleep immediately as she had been awake for sixteen hours, but only a little way into the night, she awoke, not sure what disturbed her sleep. When she had been a nursery maid, she slept lightly. She was sensitive to all noises especially the smaller ones of movement as it would indicate a wandering child. As she lay awake, she once again heard a small noise, barely distinguishable. Someone was walking in the hall on the lower floor. She went to her door and cracked it slightly, trying to catch the sound that had brought her awake. At first there was nothing, but then she heard a creak on the stairs, then another, and then a third. With a cold shiver, she realized someone was climbing the stairs, not as a quick, light-footed maid might proceed, but as one who was sneaking in a deliberately quiet fashion. Anne kept her door ajar just enough to place her cheek against it and line her eye up to watch the top of the staircase some feet away.

When the figure reached the top of the steps, Anne had to place her knuckle to her lips to prevent a gasp the prowler might hear. She recognized the wide brimmed hat and oversized outline of the painter. When he reached the top of the stairs, he did not pause for long before he turned, moving away from Anne. Her pulse pounded with the reality that he was headed towards the door to Miss Moser's room. Anne did not hear anyone coming from downstairs, and she feared that calling out might not bring help in sufficient time. She would have to take action, and it would have to be now before he entered that room.

Anne looked behind her for a weapon and spotted the pitcher standing by her basin. She took it firmly in her shaking hand and silently opened her door. The man was almost at Miss Moser's door, but still turned away from Anne. Without any concern for her safety and without much thought except to right this wrong before any harm came to the elderly artist, Anne charged the man and hit him with a full swing of the pitcher to the back of his head. The pitcher broke over his skull sending the large man forward from the blow. With a grunt and a groan, he folded under himself, landing with a thud on the floor just in the threshold of Miss Moser's room.

"What is it?" Anne heard the Mistress ask, seeing only Anne in the doorway. At the same moment Hodges arrived taking the stairs two at a time. Anne could see he carried a pistol. As the butler took in the view and saw that Anne still held the handle of a pitcher, he put an arm out to steady the girl who began to shake uncontrollably. He helped Anne to sit and took the remainder of the broken pitcher from her.

"Well, what have we here?" Hodges asked, as he lit the candle sconce on the wall. "Ah, our painter," he said to Anne with a wise smile, recalling their conversation.

"Is he dead?" Anne asked.

Miss Moser came to her door and startled at the body at her feet. She looked to Hodges for explanation.

"I believe Miss Anne has saved us all a good bit of trouble." The butler bent to the man and held a hand over his mouth, feeling the man's breath. He reached into the burglar's pocket, relieving him of a stocking wadded around a round object. Opening the sock, a rock rolled out indicating the robber's choice of a weapon.

"He is alive, but quite subdued," Hodges commented with humor.

Most of the servants had gathered at the bottom of the stairs, exchanging information as it came down to them. Hodges sent the footman off for rope. After they prepared the bundle, tying the large man's wrists and ankles and then binding those together, the two men dragged him none too carefully down the first few stairs at which point he revived, struggled, and was allowed to roll down the rest of the flight unaccompanied. The painter landed at the bottom in an awkward position having slipped once more into unconsciousness. Word was sent to the night watchman who in turn called for a constable from the end of the street where the damaged homes were being guarded. Shortly thereafter, a wagon arrived to take the man away.

Hodges dressed hurriedly and returned to find the mistress and Anne sitting in her room about to enjoy a glass of brandy.

"What a time we have had, Hodges. Poor Miss Anne must wonder at her new life in the city; first the fire, and then a burglar. I am so indebted to you, dear. There is no telling what might have occurred had you not been staying in the room down the hall."

Hodges felt more than indebtedness to the young woman. He felt very guilty that he had slept so soundly that he did not hear the intruder.

"I am afraid we were all deep in sleep due to the early morning fire. Perhaps the burglar counted on that fact. I am indeed pleased you awakened when you did to subdue the criminal. I do not know how I can express my appreciation," Hodges said with a bow to Anne.

"Well now, Miss Anne, you can no longer feel as an outsider to this household. You have become a very important part!" The elderly lady said, crossing the room to a tray with a decanter and several glasses. "You may have saved my life, and at least the trouble of dealing with a robbery or putting down the assailant. You are much to be celebrated. We must have a toast in your honor."

Miss Moser passed Anne a small crystal glass of thick amber liquid and offered one to Hodges as she took the third glass in her hand.

"Only for the toast, Ma'am," he said with a true servant's guilt.

"To Miss Anne Blake, who was sent to us by providence to protect me," Miss Moser announced, raising her glass above her head. As she lifted the glass to her lips, she looked over at Anne who seemed to have recovered from the after-affects of her daring feat.

"If you enjoyed the wine, I think you will like this even more." She winked.

4

That evening, Miss Moser's cook served a large roast with vegetables, fresh rolls, and a special cake for the occasion. Anne was surprised at such a meal prepared for two. The servants ate well here, she mused, with such a surplus. Anne was offered wine once again, and the mistress explained briefly the difference between the wine they had served the night before and the drier red wine she had chosen to accompany the beef roast. Anne listened to the details, worrying she would never completely understand the difference. She wondered if she would ever be called upon to know such things.

After dinner, Miss Moser asked Anne to sit with her awhile in her study. A nice fire warmed the room. They played a game of cards that Miss Moser taught to Anne while they talked. Anne had not played cards since she left the Duke's employ. The children had known several games. It was fun to banter and laugh with the elderly lady. After cards, Miss Moser moved to one of the two winged chairs that sat close together by the hearth.

Anne joined her on the other, easing herself back onto the tightly stuffed cushion. She was content, but she feared the feeling. She had experienced happy times before, but they had all ended with sudden and unforeseen calamity.

She would never forget how happy she had been when it was arranged for her to attend a ball. She had been elated when she opened the box from Lord Greville to reveal the soft white fabric of new gloves, gloves selected for her. She had melted when he smiled across the crowded ballroom as if they had been the only two people in the room. And yet, in all those pleasant moments she had no inkling that within hours, she would be humiliated and alone.

Later that evening, the delivery boy, Tom, would call her outside the ballroom saying something about her father. She would go to him thinking there might be an emergency. She was innocent to the idea it might be a ruse. Tom had grabbed her and forced his mouth upon hers, rubbing his groin against her, and enjoying what she had not offered. Her guilt came because she had fantasized about an encounter with this boy, but she had been blameless in the scene that Lord Greville witnessed outside the ballroom that night.

She could not excuse her involvement when the lord was injured in a scuffle with Tom, as it would never have happened had she ignored the boy's calls. She never had the opportunity to speak to the lord about that evening. Even after he returned from Wales after the death of her father, she had never clarified her relationship with Tom.

There was the moment of happiness she had felt with Lord Greville the day he had returned. It was he who did the kissing then. She had kissed him back, accepting and surrendering completely. In the end, he had shunned her, sending her to live with Miss Moser. All this had happened only weeks ago, and yet Anne felt as if it were another lifetime. No, a feeling of contentment put her on her guard. Misery was waiting just ahead. She stirred in the chair and sat upright.

"I would like to go on an outing this week," the mistress was saying, interrupting Anne's thoughts. "We will take a carriage ride, and I will show you some of the sights that we will explore more closely when spring arrives. It will be nice for you to get out and see a little of the city. I will be limited in my travels before long and unable to be a guide," she said with acceptance.

Anne looked at the lady sitting across from her in the firelight. She had grown fond of this woman in the short time they had shared. The elderly lady's face and hair were golden in the glow of the fire, making it easy for Anne to picture her as she might have looked when she was younger. The smirk of a smile on the older woman's face gave her an all-wise expression, not in a haughty way, but as a cohort of mischief. Blindness was a cruel loss to one who took such care to view the world. It seemed so unfair to Anne that she be robbed of that ability.

"I would like to take you to Kew Gardens, the Queen's cottage, to paint when the weather is better," she was thinking aloud.

"I would very much like to see a little of the town. I have never seen so many people before. The estates where I grew up were quite secluded I now realize. I have never seen houses so close together and roads so narrow. I have heard something of the gardens at Kew Palace as Lord Greville spoke of Sir Joseph Banks' work there. Many of the specimens I drew came from duplicates of those growing in Kew's hothouses."

"Ah yes, the drawings the maid destroyed. That must have been so sad for you."

"As I have said, it was a loss for Lord Greville. Some of the flowers were quite special and the depictions were an important record of their blooming." Anne only visited the drawing of the vanilla orchid for a moment before Miss Moser was asking her a new question.

"So, you worked for Lord Greville, and he paid you? Or was it understood as a payment of the expense of your boarding with your father?"

Anne squirmed in her chair again, wishing she could hide and ignore the question altogether, but she knew she should be honest and let the elderly woman know how she had come to make drawings for the lord. She avoided the subject by saying it was a short term arrangement over the blooming season before Lord Greville returned to his project at Milford.

"When Lord Greville went to Wales. Did you continue to do drawings?"

"No, I worked in the house as they had lost a maid." Anne would not tell the woman of the delivery boy, the kiss at the ball, and anymore about the maid he had run off with in the night. She hoped the lady would not ask for more clarification.

"Ah, so you were to stay on as a maid in Lord Greville's home? Why did you not do so after your father died?" Anne started to reply that it just was not meant to be, but her lips went numb, her chin quivered, and the tears pooled at the bottom of her eyes.

"Oh my dear, I have upset with these questions. I am so sorry." Miss Moser moved to the edge of her chair, waiting for the young woman to regain her composure. Taking both Anne's hands in hers and giving them a squeeze, she said, "You are a dear girl. I do not know what came to pass at the end of your stay at Lord Greville's manor, and I can say I do not care so much except to renew my promise to you. I will help you on your way as an artist, and you will never have to look back to how you arrived to be here with me. It was fate, I tell you, and I am so greatful."

Miss Moser would not delve into the poor girl's past any further though her curiosity was stirred more than when she began. Certainly, Lord Greville had not taken advantage of the girl, but he had indicated how indebted he felt to her through Sir Joseph. The lord insisted she come to Miss Moser as a student, not a maid. To think I almost said no." It had been another busy day, and Miss Moser stifled a yawn.

"I am sure you are quite tired as you were awakened so early by our uninvited guest. Let us hope we have no further incidents, fires included, so we can all get some sleep! I am so glad you were here, my dear. I cannot say that enough."

"I am thankful that I am here, also." Anne could say this with some conviction though the horizon of this latest chapter of her life loomed heavy in the distance. What would be next for her? How could she make her way alone? How long would she be able to stay with Miss Moser before she was pushed out by some uncontrollable circumstance? She could only hope that providence would provide her with the answer. Though she had suffered great sadness with each change that had come so far, she felt in some way, each new situation was somehow better than the last. Looking over at the elderly woman staring into the fire, she felt she was truly lucky.

As the lady rose and made her way to the door where Millie was waiting to assist her up the stairs, Anne had a sudden longing to hug the old woman. She reached her before she left the room. Before Anne had the chance to approach her though, the lady put her arms out to embrace her new student.

"Ah Anne, you will see, all will be well." They left the room and made their way upstairs together as a small parade of three tired women.

5

*A*s promised, Miss Moser invited Anne to take a carriage ride mid-week as a reward for her bravery and quick thinking. The weather was overcast, but dry without rain or snow. The driver was directed to make a trip through the city to point out various sights. They passed the British Museum, only blocks from Miss Moser's home, and proceeded west to the edges of the Chelsea Physic Garden, the old apothecary's garden by the river. Anne had heard of the herb garden, but had no idea of its huge size. Miss Moser pointed out Kensington Palace and she mumbled something about the Prince Regent, but Anne did not hear specifically what she said. They returned past the grounds of Westminster Hall and Abbey. The silhouette of the cathedral spires impressed Anne, and she could only imagine the splendor of the interior. Miss Moser assured her young student that they would attend a Sunday service in the abbey at some point.

They drove from Hyde Park to the Palace Gardens along the edge of Kew and back to the river. Anne marveled at the size of the city and how far they could drive without leaving it. She could control her curiosity no longer when she asked, "I wonder how far and in which direction Paddington Green is from your home?"

"Not so far, but beyond our drive today," Miss Moser answered. She would not open the wound the girl was nursing by traveling by the lord's manor. Perhaps when Anne had been given more time to unfasten the strings of her heart, she would arrange a reunion. For now, she wished she could help her young student put behind all that had occurred at nobleman's estate, but her kind heart answered, "If you look to the setting sun, that would give you an approximate direction," she added.

That was enough for Anne. She could face a sunset and know that somewhere out that way, Lord Greville continued to study his rocks, tend his flowers, and her mother's chair, the small piece of her she had left behind, sat inside a musty, damp cottage at the back edge of his property.

The elderly woman rejected any inclination for a walk as they traveled through the city. The state of the young woman's clothing was shameful. Her cloak was quite worn, and her boots, scuffed beyond repair. On the way home, however, the dame remembered she had planned to visit the apothecary's shop to pick up a waiting order. She asked if Anne might do so for her. Straining her eyes had caused her a headache, she said.

As Miss Moser sat waiting in the carriage, she recalled what she had learned of Anne's background the first evening they were together. Her mother had aided the local villagers with herbal remedies for their ailments. She had also been a midwife, delivering several of the Duke's nieces, nephews, and grandchildren. Anne's mother, as well as her younger brother, had died during the epidemic in 1801, leaving Anne with her father, an undergardener at the Duke's estate. When her father went to work for Lord Greville, he had left his daughter behind at the wishes of the Duke's daughters. They took her in, and Anne became a nursery maid at a very young age. She accompanied the children to their schoolroom and had taken advantage of the education. It was remarkable to know Anne had come from such a lowly birth to be such an accomplished young lady. Anyone who met her would not place her in such a station, but those clothes, Miss Moser sighed to herself.

She felt Anne might be interested in seeing an apothecary's shop as she knew Anne had an interest and some knowledge in herbs. There were several apothecary establishments in London. These shops and the men who ran them were now accepted as reputable medical advisers. Miss Moser used the shop owned and operated by the Parkers, father and son. The elderly lady utilized several eye washes, a skin tonic, salves, and tinctures for all sorts of ailments that she procured from the Parker's shop.

"Here we are, Anne. Just tell Mr. Parker that you are picking up my order for me. I have an account, so no money need change hands."

Anne was amused to see the apothecary's sign was a coltsfoot plant, drawn with both leaves and flowers as it never occurred in nature. The leaves came first and then later it bloomed, but the leaves and flowers never appeared on the plant together. She had drawn the flower when she first came to live with her father, and she had later spoken with Lord Greville about its use for her father's lung condition. Everywhere she looked she was reminded of the lord and her past life.

The afternoon she had been caught harvesting herbs and flowers in the lord's garden was deeply embarrassing. After all, she had been caught trespassing in his library before that. The nobleman had assured her he did not mind her taking herbs from his garden. Anne had been very surprised how Lord Greville commented with familiarity about the use of certain plants much as a country layman might have. When she spoke of her mother, Lord Greville had been so kind.

The lord had been so considerate to her that day. But that was before the dance and her impropriety of leaving the ballroom, and certainly before the death of her father and the kiss she had shared with the lord a mere month ago. She stopped her thoughts, angry at the incessant progression. Would she never stop thinking of everything in terms of her time with Lord Greville?

Anne stepped down into the little shop that sat lower than the street level. In the window was a display of bottles, tins, soaps, and bath salts. Dried herbs were arranged around the window sill in an appealing display. As she opened the door, she was met with the strong odor of all that was for sale within. The heady combination of pungent leaves, sweet flowers, camphor and alcohol came like a strong wave almost bowling Anne over in the stone doorway. As she swung the door open wider, the scents rushed past her to the outdoors.

A small bell on the back side of the door jingled as she closed the door. Inside the shop, it was darker and closer. Rows of shelves filled with bottles, stacks of boxes and tins took up one wall, and two tall cabinets of small drawers filled the opposite wall. Behind the counter, oriental jars, corked pottery, and rows of gradient glass bottles stood in perfect lines halfway up the wall. Anne stood in wonder at the display. The odor of the place condensed into an even stronger scent mixed with the new smell of oak cabinets. Anne felt it was a worldly smell. Some of the spices would have come from far away. Some of the herbs might have come from an open field at the edge of town, or perhaps the apothecary harvested some from one of the gardens she had seen that morning. A young man stood up from behind the counter. He gave Anne a once-over glance, noticing she dressed as a servant, not a customer.

"Can I help you, Miss?" the young man asked. He looked with a sideways glance and a furrowed brow, questioning her presence in the shop. Bottles were missing, and he had decided to keep a closer eye on all who entered. When Anne turned toward him, he was surprised at how lovely she was. Her skin was clear, her eyes, intense. She smiled in a way he found difficult to resist finding pleasant. She was lovely to look upon, housemaid or not.

"Yes, I am here to pick up Miss Moser's order," Anne replied plainly to the handsome clerk. He stood several inches taller than she. He had broad shoulders, but a thin waist. His head held a thick crop of light brown hair the top of which shone in the light coming through the row of windows along the front wall. His cheeks were ruddy, and his brown eyes matched his hair perfectly, not dark but auburn. Her heart beat quickened as she found his appearance was agreeable. She realized she was staring. He met her stare with one of his own. Anne looked down quickly, pretending to examine the contents of the boxes in front of her.

Though the young man thought the maid very pretty, he was not one to be taken in too easily. "Do you have the lady's card or some indication as to your connection with Miss Moser?" he asked stiffly.

"I am her student," Anne answered immediately.

"Her student, how is that?" He asked with a scorn to his voice.

"I am under her tutelage in painting," Anne replied proudly, ignoring his tone. She could tell the man doubted as much, and he was not going to give her the package.

Anne saw that he balked, and so she added, with some annoyance, "Do you doubt me, Sir?" His expression and his delay in producing the package told her as much. "Miss Moser is waiting in the carriage outside, if you wish to speak to her," Anne pointed out.

The store clerk went to the window. He saw Miss Moser waiting outside as the pretty maid said. He supposed he could give the woman the package despite her tale about being an art student.

Anne was miffed at his hesitation. She thought to ask for the apothecary, but she would not cause this clerk trouble if he was going to relent. The man brought down the items from the shelf behind the counter. The order was neatly wrapped in brown paper with Miss Moser's name on the slip tied to the bundle. As he placed them on the counter, Anne snatched up the package and stomped out of the shop indignantly. She supposed in this city, no one trusted each other. It disturbed her that the shopkeeper accused her of lying.

Though the young apothecary tried to hop around the counter to get the door for the maid, he did not reach it in time, catching his hip on the corner. The girl marched out and never looked back. He found he was quite perturbed and in pain as he rubbed his hip. Whoever did she think she was? He asked himself.

An older man emerged from the back room after hearing the slam of the front door. "Who was that?" he asked.

"I cannot say," his son replied, still rubbing his side. "A maid who came to retrieve Miss Moser's order."

"Was there a problem?" he asked, curious about the bang of the door.

"No problem that we must concern ourselves with," his son replied, trying to forget his prejudice and how the young woman seemed to put him in his place instead.

James Parker shared his business with his son, John. They knew each of their patients well and were in good standing in the community. He did not wish for any misunderstandings with a customer. They might seek another apothecary. He would let the matter go, but he did think his son a bit standoffish at times and hoped he had not caused any ill will. Now, as he watched his son, he saw he was unusually distracted. John was standoffish, yes, even-keeled, always. Whoever this maid was had certainly disturbed him.

John was agitated. He had never had a woman look at him with such defiance. She really thought she was somebody, but her manner of dress spoke otherwise. That story about being a student, well her lies would catch up with her. It was not for him to sort out. He was ashamed at himself for giving it such attention.

6

*O*n Thursday, as the mistress had planned, the dress fitting took place in Miss Moser's room. Anne felt the blush on her cheeks rise as the dress maker ran her tape around various parts of her body. The seamstress had shared private comments with Miss Moser, and she noticed her opinion had not been sought. It did not concern her as the pleasure of having new clothes was so much stronger. These dresses would be very special as they would be made specifically for her. She had worn only hand-me-downs since the death of her mother.

When Anne first took her old worn wool uniform off, the dress maker raised her eyebrows, no doubt at the condition of the young girl's chemise. Anne had only two undergarments. She hand-washed one daily, and they were worn to threads, patched in the underarms, and had been hemmed to above her knee. Knowing this fitting was to come, Anne had taken special care to clean the better of the two. She also requested a scrap of material from the rag bag Mrs. Holgate kept in the back hallway. Anne found a tablecloth with a large hole in the middle, blackened and stiff with wax. It was obvious some mishap with a candle had sent the cloth to the ragbag. She cut two long strips from along the sides of the burnt area.

Anne basted and sewed together crude legs and pants to form a pantaloon, a garment she had seen the duchesses wearing when she had been in their employ. As the seamstress lifted her chemise to take a peek, she was further surprised to see Anne's creation. With that view, she called to Miss Moser who was busy reading letters at her desk in the corner. The two murmured a conversation. Anne could not hear what was said, but the dress maker was asking questions, and Miss Moser was all assurances and agreement as far as Anne could tell.

When the fitting was completed and the seamstress had departed, Anne and her mentor took tea together which had become a custom when the mistress was home and not entertaining others. Anne watched carefully as the teapot arrived with two cups, a bowl of sugar, and a small pitcher of milk. The mistress added the milk to her own cup and a spoon of sugar to Anne's. Anne had served her father's tea in a mug with as much sugar as they could spare. She had come to like her tea sweet, but had lessened her desire for sweetness partially because she did not wish to extend the expense she cost the elderly woman.

After the tea was added to their cups, Millie would take the pot to a side tray and add more water, placing a cover over the pot. This second cup was always weaker. Anne preferred it to the stronger taste of this first cup. Perhaps the ritual relaxed her, and she was better able to enjoy that second cup.

Miss Moser stirred her tea and milk together without a sound. A simple waving back and forth of the spoon and then she would place the spoon on the right side of her saucer. Anne imitated the stirring motion. She waved her spoon through the pale brown liquid silently, careful not to hit the sides of the cup. She watched as the circling, swimming sugar crystals disappeared. She placed her spoon down exactly as Miss Moser had shown, whereupon conversation began.

"I hope you will come to accept your arrival here, and not look back too harshly at what has gone on in the past." Miss Moser was thinking of Anne's comments the evening before. You are here now, and that has turned out to be quite the blessing."

Miss Moser had not asked Sir Joseph about Lord Greville's relationship with the young woman, but she had a sense that something had happened between them for which the lord felt Anne must find a position elsewhere. What he did instead was seek out lessons for her. Miss Moser had agreed, compelled by Anne's drawings.

Mary Moser knew the history of Lord Greville's mistress, Emma Hamilton, the woman he had taken in and refined. The beauty had been Romney's pet. There were paintings of her in a variety of poses and costumes. Greville had sent his mistress to his uncle in Naples while trying to find a wife with a fortune. It was an old story now replaced by the tales of Emma's relationship with Admiral Nelson and the sea hero's death. What Miss Moser did not know was Anne's history, and she thought to ease into that subject. She wished to know Anne better and get to the bottom of the sadness she saw so often in her eyes.

"You were living with your father at Lord Greville's Paddington manor waiting for a position as a nursery maid before coming here, is that correct?

"Yes. I was a nursery maid for the Duke's family."

"How long did you live with them?" Most of her eighteen years, the girl had replied. How sad that separation must have been. The elderly woman looked at Anne with a new fondness as she continued her story.

"My father came to work for Lord Geville six years ago after my mother and brother died. I stayed on until I was sent to live with my father nine months ago."

"So you waited for a new situation, but it never came? What did you do in the interim?"

Anne worried about this line of questioning as it was going to drag her through what she had wished to forget. The lady meant well she was sure, but she could not endure telling the whole tale.

"I waited for a letter of recommendation from Lady Henrietta, or a new situation she sought for me. Neither came to be. I am afraid I overstepped my curiosity and was caught in Lord Greville's library. That is when he set me to task for the trespass by drawing his flowering plants in the hothouse."

"Why did you enter the lord's library?" Miss Moser felt sure the young woman had her reasons.

"It is difficult to explain," Anne began. She felt uncomfortable sharing the subject with Miss Moser, though she knew the lady would not judge her. She still thought of her view of the lord as a private matter; one she had never described to anyone except in a brief conversation with Lord Greville's cook. If she were to break that confidence, surely no one was more appropriate than the elderly woman sitting across from her who had shown her nothing but kindness.

"I witnessed Lord Greville in distress the first day he returned from Wales. I wished to understand his emotions." There it was, out in the open; a statement of an event of which she had sworn never to speak.

"So, you witnessed his lordship upset and you had empathy for him. That is not so difficult to understand. Entering his library, however, that was well beyond your boundaries. I suppose you know that now."

Yes and no, Anne thought to herself. After all that came to pass with the lord, they had become friends because of that trespass whereas if she had remained out of sight as she should have, she might never have met the lord, and her current situation would have been altogether different. She could not regret her entry into the library that day even if her heart ached for all that came about because of it. She pondered a reply, but chose to say nothing.

"I believe there is more. Perhaps your time spent with Lord Greville accounted for more?"

A pang of fear crept up from Anne's stomach to her throat. She had said too much and now must put an end to this chain of questions that would only lead back to misery, a kiss, and being sent to live with the artist who now questioned her.

"No, it is sad the drawings were lost, but a record of the plants and their blooms was important to his lordship. I was happy to be occupied."

Miss Moser could see the girl's fingers writhed together. She had hit a nerve and once again her questions had caused the girl some discomfort. She would pry no further.

"The dress maker is pleased to make these new dresses for you. I have ordered some accessories as well. I do not want to hear any complaints about money spent or my indulgence. These purchases will make your appearance as my companion more appropriate."

Anne heard the word "companion" out of all that the elderly lady said. She had been shocked to find out she was to be a student here and not a maid. The idea of being the lady's companion carried with it much more than a descriptive term. It would be a considerable leg up in society. No longer would she be several tiers below the lady. She would be accepted on the edge of all of society under such a title. Miss Moser could take a student several places in her world. She could take "her companion" everywhere.

"Unfortunately, they will not be ready in time to accompany me to the opening of the season and this year's display at the Royal Academy."

Anne knew nothing of the gala events that usually announced the beginning of the season. She preferred not to think of attending any of these affairs. Once she received her new clothes she could only hope the mistress would not require her to appear publicly too quickly. It all was a little frightening especially when she thought of those in Society who had only caused her woe. She had no desire to overlap with any of them.

"I truly appreciate your kindness. I hope I can fit into the role you have chosen for me as well as fitting into the clothes you have purchased to do so." Anne sipped the last of her tea and returned the cup to the saucer as carefully as her nervous hand would allow. She wished to retreat to her room and the solace of no more questions. The lady had every right to know her past, but it continued to wound her every time she was forced to speak of it.

Miss Moser heard the humility in Anne's voice once more. Though she had not discovered the source of this low self-worth, she knew she was putting together a picture of a lonely little girl who had been tossed about by members of the nobility. As Miss Moser had no fondness for class structure and how it controlled lives, she, herself, had come through it well. She had her father to thank for her ability to move through society as she had. For Anne, Miss Moser felt an injustice had been meted on a sweet person. When Anne accepted her talents and abilities and blossomed into a most accomplished and unique woman because of her background, Miss Moser intended to be there to watch. Time and new experiences would heal the wounds the young woman kept inside.

"I feel you are already a part of my life, Anne. I hope you will come to think of your life here as an equal part of it. I am so happy you came to us."

Was it the way the lady addressed her with such heartfelt language or was it the tone of her voice, soft and nurturing? Whatever it was, Anne felt she could trust this woman and the offer of happiness here. Anne felt a huge weigh float up from her heart and soul as she curtsied her way out of the matron's room. Before she was out the door, she ran back in to open arms and a shared hug.

Miss Moser dabbed a tear, sensing a new beginning for Anne.

7

The light of morning was streaming in through a crack in the drapes as Anne woke up to an unusually quiet city. Looking out the window, she understood why. Everything in her view was covered with a layer of snow. It was still snowing. The landscape was a pretty sight. The snow was sticking to each window ledge on the row of houses across the street. Each part of the iron fences which ran along the front of the homes was outlined in white, and each point softened by a white snow ball on top.

Anne had not accustomed herself to the crowded city as of yet. She felt the way the buildings stood connected together in rows was confining. The conversations of neighbors she could hear on each side made her uncomfortable. The bustle in the street for most of the day distracted her. The snowy blanket that draped over everything muffled the sounds of the few carriages passing on the street below, and this view of their street was the prettiest yet.

Anne hurried to dress, taking her boots with her downstairs. She slipped through the kitchen giving Mrs. Holgate and the kitchen maids a start.

"Good morning," she said to the housekeeper, as she continued through the kitchen. Anne yanked on her boots, and wrapped her shawl around her shoulders tightly, then stepped out into the falling flakes. She stood looking out over Miss Moser's tiny garden, thinking of her father. One month had passed since his death and her move to this place. She looked out, picturing another garden as her thoughts went to Lord Greville. Heartache came quickly as she allowed the icy kisses of snowflakes land on her cheeks, melting and joining a few hot tears that traveled down her face.

The snow coated the bushes, forming layers of white and dark green. The sky was changing as the snow stopped. Its rosy color was reflected off all the white surfaces changing the white world to pink. Anne thought she might try to paint the scene.

She ran back in the house to the chastisement of Mrs. Holgate. "You will catch a chill, Miss."

"I know, but it is so beautiful," Anne replied. She took her boots off and carried them across the kitchen floor so as not to leave wet tracks. The hem of her dress was wet, and her socks were soaked through. She informed Mrs. Holgate she would return to her room before breakfast to change. The cook replied that it was still early and Mistress was not awake as of yet. "Packages came for you, Miss," she added.

Coming into her bedroom, Anne saw several boxes had arrived and took up the entire end of her bed. Her new clothes had arrived. There were many boxes, not at all what she expected. Anne wondered what could be in so many packages.

It was a treasure trove of clothing. Two boxes contained shoes, new pale blue slippers, and a new pair of boots. The first dress box contained a long sleeved dress of what she guessed was thin wool. It was the color of milk, very plain with a high collar and only a small gathered trim of lace at the end of the sleeves. It would be warm, but not as heavy or itchy as the dark blue uniform she had on. The next box contained a pure white muslin bound with a light blue ribbon about the waist and a small blue gathered collar and straight long sleeves. It was elegant. She was amazed to think she would be allowed to wear such a beautiful gown.

The third dress box held a short sleeve dress of thick cotton printed with a pattern of pale gray leaves on a white background. It was fitted with a pale green-grey sash just below the bust and then hung loosely from there. The short sleeves were gathered with the same color ribbon woven into the gathering. It was beautifully simple, but so special. And it was hers. It was so much prettier than anything Anne had ever known. Even the dresses of the Duke's ladies had not been as beautifully made as these gowns.

Before Anne would try on her new dresses, she looked into the other boxes. The last of the large boxes contained a pelisse in light grey with pearlescent buttons. Anne could not believe her eyes. Her grey cape had sufficed for so long. She had never owned anything so tailored to her dimensions.

She looked through the remaining packages, anxious to try on her clothes. One small box held several pairs of stockings. A medium box contained three chemises of fine cotton and a petticoat hemmed with a narrow strip of lace. She imagined it would look well under the short sleeved dress. She had never had a petticoat. It would protect the hem of her dress if she were out in the damp or mud. As Anne stacked the boxes she had opened to the side, she opened the last smaller one to find undergarments. The very last box must hold a hat, she guessed.

Removing the lid, she discovered a straw bonnet. It was just the sort of bonnet she had always wanted. It had a decoration of blue ribbon around the top, and it tied under the chin. She ran to her mirror to model the new hat and then saw her ugly navy blue dress staring back.

She shed her old dress, leaving it in a neglected pile by the dresser and then went back to try a new dress. When she looked at her reflection, she saw her old shift hung haphazardly from her thin body. She pulled off the remainder of her clothes and began to reach for her new chemise when she thought better of it.

Pouring chilled water into her basin, she washed her body from neck to toes until she began to shiver. Drying herself quickly, she finally felt it was fitting to put on her new clothes.

She tried each dress with the pelisse and found they fit so correctly that she could admire her shape for the first time. She had lost weight while at Lord Greville's. The plumpness of a nursery maid's life had worn off with worry and hard work. She would be careful to not overeat as these clothes fit her present size so exactly.

She stared at the pile of garments on her bed. She thought of the cost, and again her thoughts wandered to Lord Greville. In clothes such as these, would he have been so ready to send her away? She checked her anger as she decided to wear the new wool dress down to breakfast as she was sure Miss Moser would want her to do. She laughed at how changed was the girl who went out in the snow to the one who stared back from the mirror, now. This fine lady's companion was someone new. It was Hodges who saw her first when she came downstairs.

"If I may say, Miss Anne, you look lovely this morning." He did not specify the new clothes, though he most likely knew of them. He made Anne feel like any woman feels who is noticed by someone she admires. When the mistress arrived, she drew a breath as she said, "Oh, one of your new dresses. What a pleasing picture you make." Anne looked exquisite, she commented to herself. Her eyes met Hodges' who gave her a nod of approval. It was amazing how changed Anne appeared from the housemaid in the heavy, navy-blue wool dress. "How do you like them, Anne?"

"I have never worn anything as nice. And to think, they are mine," she said innocently. She would accept the splendor of new clothes as her part of the bargain. The lady's art instruction of course was a part. If she were to be sent away from Miss Moser's care, she would at least have new clothes to take with her.

Anne's speech and manners did not reflect her birth status. Now her appearance was such that no one would believe she had come to be Miss Moser's companion through anything other than the usual channels as a relative of a friend, not as a gardener's daughter.

"Today, you will need to wear an apron over your new dress," the lady encouraged. As these clothes fit well, we can order you other necessary gowns; walking dresses, evening gowns, and perhaps a ball gown."

"Oh, I could not attend a ball, Ma'am. I have no desire to attend any such function. I would rather not," she stuttered with fear.

Miss Moser was surprised. "Why ever not, dear?"

"I had the chance to attend a dance in Westbourne last September. I am grateful for your thoughtfulness, but I do not long for such social outings."

"Well, if the occasion should arise, I might want you to accompany me. You could stay at my side if you wished. Perhaps you have not had the chance to learn the steps, my apologies," the matron added, realizing the girl's possible embarrassment.

"No, I am able to perform the patterns. I accompanied my charges to dancing lessons and we practiced often enough that I had fun at the dance last fall."

"Then what bothers you so?" Miss Moser asked.

Anne paused as she considered how to answer the lady's question. Honestly, she decided. She would like Miss Moser to know.

"I was called outside by the grocer's delivery boy. He said he had some news from my father. It was wrong of me to go out alone."

"Ah, of course it would have been better to have been escorted, but you returned to the dance shortly after a conversation with the boy?"

"Unfortunately, not. He grabbed me and forced a kiss upon me that I did not solicit."

"Oh my. Did you call out for help?"

"Lord Greville arrived before I was able to alert anyone. He saw the kiss and misunderstood, thinking I had some part in the meeting."

"So, you fear that you would do so again," the matron asked cleverly.

"No. Never! I would never make such a mistake again." Anne shook her head vehemently with her statement.

"Well, then what is your worry? You have learned your lesson. You have not permanently damaged your reputation. No one knows of the incident, so you have nothing to trouble you except that as I say, you may have a difficult time making your excuses to those who would wish to dance with you." Miss Moser smiled and chuckled to herself. Indeed many a young man would find Anne's innocent manner refreshing. The elderly woman was aware that Anne was not so sophisticated that she could be coy. No, it would be necessary to protect her to some degree and be sure to prevent any such occurrence to ever happen again.

Anne wondered that she had never had the chance to explain the scene at the dance to anyone until now. She felt relieved, and to think the lady made so light of it.

"I would do as you wished, but as I say, I have no need of such entertainment," Anne reaffirmed with less conviction than before.

8

nne slipped on an apron and carefully rolled back the sleeves of her new dress. She had thought to put on one of her old dresses, but Miss Moser had resisted.

"I want you to take those garments to Mrs. Marshall. She will see that they are put in the rag bag. I don't want to see those dowdy old things again," she quipped.

Anne went to the table for a new sheet of paper. Miss Moser had requested she look out the front window and down the street to sketch the rows of houses on each side. The exercise was a lesson in perspective, teaching Anne how the size of objects diminished as they progressed further away.

Miss Moser stood in front of the window pointing to the buildings. "See how colorful the details in these first houses are. Even the color of the snow has more definition."

Nodding her head slightly, Anne could see that.

Then the teacher pointed to the railings that ran along the road and how they were parallel with the roof lines at the top. She indicated with the tilt of her hand how as the view traveled back down the street, these parallel lines were drawn with a slant to indicate their diminishing.

Anne looked more closely at the street scene and saw that by the time the end of the street would go off the paper, the view would be quite narrow.

"It is most important to learn to frame your scene before you begin to sketch. If you start your drawing with say, the door of that house there," she said, pointing across the street and one house down, "then you must keep it small enough to include more of the view down the street. If you make the house too big, that will be that, and you will paint a very nice picture of that house, and nothing more. She smiled at Anne with her explanation. She knew Anne was already aware of framing, but this was the lesson in its entirety as she had taught it so many times before.

With that, she left Anne to begin her sketch of the street scene.

Anne finished the sketch in an hour, peeking out the window to recall the details of the window casings and doorways. She had included a man and his wagon on the north side of the street. The delivery was completed in less than an hour, so Anne was forced to draw much of the horse from memory.

When Miss Moser returned and looked over Anne's shoulder, she was pleased to see the girl's diligence. As her teacher, she had not asked Anne to include activity in the street, and yet the girl had taken on many of the morning's activities in her drawing. The planters on the porch of the house on the south side of the road and the cart and horse opposite, made the picture so much more interesting even if the drawing was only an exercise. Quite unique, Miss Moser thought, amazed at her pupil's ability.

"I think you are ready to paint," the mistress found herself saying. Usually painting was held over the heads of students as a reward for completing these exercises, sometimes two and three times. Not so with this pupil. Miss Moser would not require the young woman to sketch a box or a staircase, two of the more tedious perspective assignments. There was no use wasting time. Anne's ability to recreate what she saw was so advanced that there would be no need to repeat any of the lessons.

"The sketch you have made is quite charming and deserves some color if you would like. You will work with watercolors for this exercise, but when you are ready, I wish for you to take on an oil painting. You must think of the subject you might depict. Oils are so rewarding though they must be executed in the studio. The watercolors are so much easier to portage outdoors. We will be traveling to do so in the parks soon, as weather permits."

Miss Moser slid a large wooden box out from the side of her chair. Anne marveled at the selection of colors the artist offered to her to use. It contained rows of colors in rectangular shapes, some more worn at one edge than others. The mistress retrieved several small porcelain trays from a drawer. She then brought out a long box of brushes. Behind them, Millie was busy pouring water into a pan in which they would wet the paper. Wetting the paper would allow the water-based paints to adhere and absorb into the paper.

Anne knew of this process as she had wet much of the paper she used when rendering flower drawings for Lord Greville. She had found she could only do so once. Rewetting inferior papers caused deterioration of the surface. Pilling would occur if too much water came to the paper with subsequent brush strokes. She had no doubt Miss Moser's paper supply would be of the most superior grade.

Miss Moser selected a small handful of brushes from the box. "These are mostly sable brushes. They are made from the fur of an animal that lives where it is very cold, developing long hairs. The hairs are sorted and brought together to form a brush with a pointed or rounded tip." She looked up to see Anne was intent on the brushes she was running through the tips of her fingers. "I have used other furs; wolf, squirrel, and even skunk as in this one here." She passed Anne a black and white haired brush which did look as if it had come from a skunk to Anne. She smiled to think of it.

"It is the important requirement of these watercolor brushes to deliver the paint in a fashion useful to the artist. For covering a wide band with color, one would use this brush." Miss Moser chose another brush from the box. The end was shaped like a fan. "These are Japanese brushes; they work well for large areas of color." She passed Anne the brush. As Anne ran her finger over hairs of the brush, she found it was softer than it looked and as the lady had said, must hold a great deal of paint.

"For detail work and fine lines, this brush," she said, passing Anne the smallest brush in the box. "Its tip was very fine. The fine hair of the sable, when initially wet, forms into a tight circle from which the finest lines can be made." She dipped her fingers into a tray of water Millie had prepared and rolled the end of the brush into a point. "These brushes are called "riggers" because they can be used to paint the finest lines such as the lines of a ship's ropes." Anne mimicked the lady's pinch on the end of the brush. Anne felt the brush's hairs twine together until only one hair stood out a fraction above the rest.

"I considered a sable collar and cuff on a dress once, symbolic of the animals who give their fur to brush making. So many would not have understood my meaning, and I thought the appearance was too aristocratic for my blood," the lady teased. Anne noticed Miss Moser often spoke with an undertone of disapproval when she referred to the nobility. Anne wondered if she had been chastised by that sector at some point. No doubt her very open affair with the married miniature artist, Richard Cosway, might have caused gossip. Anne remembered hearing about the affair from Cook when she first knew Anne was being sent to live with the aging artist. Perhaps that was where Miss Moser's aversion to the upper crust had its roots.

As the elderly artist examined each brush, she laid it in a slanted tray of water. "Keeping the brushes from drying between colors is more important when we begin oils, but I use the tray for water also. This pot of water will suffice for cleaning, but we do not leave the brushes sitting where their tips become bent. Here is a pitcher of clean water for mixing. When you are finished, wash up your brushes for the last time, roll the tips as I have shown you, and place them handle down in the pot to dry."

"Most of these brushes are far too delicate for using with oils. We will use brushes such as these for your work with oils." She turned toward her maid, but Millie was already bringing the teacher another wooden box, longer than the previous one. Inside was another selection of brushes, carefully stored in separate compartments. She brought out three of the brushes to show Anne. Millie removed the heavy box from her mistress' lap, but stood by watching.

"These are made from hog bristles. The surface of an oil painting requires a construction that can withstand the rough surface of the canvas and the stiffer consistency of the oils." Anne felt the tips and was surprised by the stiffness of the hairs. Such a different tool for a method she had yet to try. Returning the brushes to their spots in the box, Millie returned the box to the table beside the desk.

"You will begin your painting with your washes. This is another brush you might use for this first step." She placed a wide flat cut brush in the tray. "You must also consider if there is to be any white in the painting. That must be decided now."

Anne studied her drawing as the wet surface gleamed back at her. Millie had tacked it to a board so that it could not curl. Anne's pencil drawing showed through. The sky was white, the snow on the railings was white, and the piles here and there along the street were white, though they showed dark edges where there was now dirt and soot. Even these white areas had a grey tone, but she could leave the bit open until she painted in the details. Anne was aware of how difficult it was to blot the paper back to white.

Miss Moser had Millie wet two scraps of paper and pass them to Anne. "A place to examine your colors. I would recommend that you paint the closest buildings first after your wash, then, as you move down the street, you will add water as needed to indicate distance with the fading colors. The cart and flowers would be your last areas to paint and their detail and color will be the strongest. It will be a pretty scene."

Miss Moser sat at her desk. She poured a small amount of water into one of the porcelain trays. She chose the black rectangle closest to her in the box. It was marked with the words, "Bone Black". She wet the pigment in the box and then replaced her brush in the tray of water. Anne watched as the paint spread out into the water. The color was very black and did not disperse to be anything but black, not grey at all. Her teacher painted a stroke on the paper and then looked up. "Oh," she said with a new thought. She took a larger rectangle of pigment from a drawer. "I have not painted with watercolors in such a long time, I almost forgot. Now you try this one."

Anne dipped her brush in the water and then into the small box, wiping the dry block with the wet tip of the brush until she saw the dark color travel up the hairs. When she returned the brush to the water, the color panned out to grey rather than staying so purely black.

Miss Moser took up the paper. Anne painted the last color on it, noticing how the brush spread the black to a blue grey in a short distance. "Quite a difference?" Miss Moser indicated she try the Bone Black, and Anne saw that it stayed black as she drug the brush across the paper.

"Very black," Miss Moser said. "It would be a good choice for the railings. The other is a gift from my friend, William Payne. He mixes three paints to make this one. I have used it for sketching as well. It is an excellent wash color for the sky and for water."

"Is it true the Bone Black is made from burnt bones?" Anne asked.

"Yes, it is made from animal bones from the slaughter house. Once a long time ago, in Egypt, a special paint was made from the wrappings of mummies. I can only imagine some symbolism was connected with the use of the brown coloring as a celebration of the afterlife, a favorite topic of the pharoahs." She raised her eyebrows as she explained. Anne made a grimace.

"I am glad I do not have to worry about the use of such paints," Anne said.

"Most paints are mined minerals. There are some more toxic than those I choose to use. I avoid the paints declared poisonous, but it is best not to get the paint on your skin."

Miss Moser stood as Millie helped her remove her apron. "Enjoy my paints, dear. For now, I will rest before tea." The woman left the studio with her maid who had watched and listened to all Miss Moser had instructed with keen attention. It was suddenly quiet. Anne looked around feeling very privileged to be left alone to work in Miss Moser's studio.

She chose the black that readily merged out into the water. With a little more water, it thinned to a grey-blue. Anne went to the window to look at the sky for the oddities of misty clouds she would try to represent. Closer to the horizon, just over the roofs of the buildings, the sky was darker. Anne began the wash on her paper. As she worked her way down the page, through buildings, and onto the street, she increased the color and left the area of white above the scene where fog was forming in the distance and a place where the clouds would be.

As she worked down the sides of the buildings on the street, she added the tiniest bit of brown. She had tried one brown which was similar to the one she had in her own paint set. It was too brown. The next brown she chose was redder, the color of dirt, which suited her purpose as the road came closer in the view. Her curiosity about the colors had been peaked by Miss Moser's instruction about the black pigments. She would ask about the browns as she knew there would be stories to go with the names Sepia, Umber, and Sienna. Anne imagined they had something to do with their Italian sounding names.

An hour and a half later, the background was dry and so she was able to paint the edges of the buildings carefully. Anne did not to allow the color to blend, keeping the edges sharp. She was ready to paint in the last details. She started at the end of the street as her teacher had instructed. Anne tried the delicate brush. She held it tightly between her index finger and her middle finger as she dragged the side of her hand along, concentrating on making the fine black line of the railings as straight as possible.

At first she used the grey timidly, forming shadows in the snow piled along the side of the houses. As she worked down the view, coming closer, she added a bit of blue and found the color truly reflected the afternoon's sky in day old snow. With the addition of the wrought iron work intermittently showing through the snow, she began to see that she had captured not only the view that day, but also the feeling of the cold on the city's street. She would never forget this day.

Looking out the window at the current activity, no deliveries and only one couple walking in the lane, she looked back at her painting. The feeling was much the same. Just as the depiction was two dimensional, her life here in this busy city was similar. She saw her reflection in the window as an overlay of the scene. She was not a part of any of it. A lonely sadness was about to overtake her when the door opened and Miss Moser entered.

It was almost tea time. Anne had no idea it was so late, though the light out the window was fading from the mid-day brightness. Much of the snow was gone. She had the cart and the horse's details to finish. Anne had worried about recreating the harness and reins as her model was no longer present. With the addition of a passerby, she was able to cover her need to show the details of the horse's equipage. The flowers out front of the houses were a focal point on the painting and the last part she would paint. She imagined they must be bulbs, so bright in the late winter.

Her mentor came around behind her to bend closer to the painting. Everywhere Miss Moser looked on the paper, she could see Anne had put the correct perspective and fading colors to the buildings, the street, and the sky in the distance. Above and beyond the lesson, Anne's painting was a charming view of the city.

She wished she had seen more of the girl's previous work. She had only the two timid paintings she had received from Lord Greville. They barely revealed Anne's style. It was evident here. There was a softness to her renderings. This painting held more confidence, but still a certain timidity. She stood and clapped her hands together. "Very nice, Anne. I am very pleased with your progress. I don't think we need wait any longer to move on to using the oil paints."

For the first time, Anne took pride in her creation. The exercise had been a challenge, but she felt she had met the difficulty without the self-doubt she had suffered while painting for Lord Greville. Miss Moser patted her shoulder, "Enough for today or your eyes will be as sore as mine!" She waited for the young woman to clean her brushes and remove her apron and then arm in arm they went to her parlor for tea.

9

*A*nne watched the daylight hours grow longer as they headed toward springtime. With the longer days, time seemed to pass more slowly. Her time was busy enough with lessons in the studio, but all in all, the cadence of life was so unhurried it had begun to be dull. Anne appreciated the break from the chaos of her move to live with the artist and her hard life as a maid, but there was little to her life outside this house, an oasis in a very crowded and busy city.

She saw people out the windows, hurrying to and fro. Carriages delivered goods and neighbors to the adjacent houses, yet she knew none of these people. She could not count the household staff as friends, they stayed to themselves, treating her as a relative to Miss Moser rather than the housemaid she had once been.

Sensing her uneasiness, Miss Moser had taken her to several historic sites, but mostly to be viewed from the carriage windows. They had seen the Tower of London and so many palaces, Anne had quite forgotten who lived where, except that the King and his family were currently at Kew Palace. Anne loved the thought that the mistress was so familiar with the royals, but she was ashamed that her own knowledge of the monarchy was so rusty. Anne found a book in Miss Moser's library to review her country's history. From the Henrys' famous reigns to the revolution in America and the ever-present threat of France, there was much upon which to reflect, but no one with whom she could discuss the events.

Bits of news came to her about the new country formed from British colonies so far across the Atlantic. Wealthy merchants as well as poor Irish families were making the journey across the ocean in hope of a new start. She heard tales of the land's vast territories as reported by the explorers, Lewis and Clark. Anne wondered at the horizons there. The thought that one could look out and see nothing but wilderness was appealing. She had not accepted the city life of London, and her heart ached for an emptier view.

Miss Moser expressed her regret that she must attend certain social events in the evening, leaving Anne alone for her meals. There were also the afternoons when Anne stayed upstairs in the studio as visitors came for tea. Anne could hear them laugh and sometimes hear bits of their lively conversation. On two occasions, the lady attended afternoon meetings. At another time, she went to a tea at another artist's home.

All this exclusion improved Anne's diligence. She would make something of her life. The opportunity she had been given would not go to waste. Anne did not expect more from her situation, and in no way blamed the mistress, once again fitting between but not within the society with whom she spent most of her time.

The rain was incessant. It had rained most of the last two weeks, and when it wasn't raining, it was foggy, dreary, or so dark and gloomy, one would think it the end of the world. Anne worked by the window where the natural light still came through the overcast sky better than the lamplight could provide. She had started a sketch for her first oil painting. Miss Moser had advised a still life, encouraging Anne to arrange a group of objects as a model.

As Anne looked about to begin her arrangement, she spotted the cat, Edward. He was curled into a tight spiral on the small green and white striped loveseat at the other end of the big windows. The arm of the sofa curved around him. On a small marble-topped table beside the couch was a white porcelain vase of daffodils. Each dark green stem held the skirted cup of a radiant yellow flower. The scene was perfect without moving a thing.

Edward looked up as if he knew he was to be the subject of her painting. She sketched quickly, fearful he would move, but he settled back down in seconds. Anne had drawn several positions of the cat as he was sitting, cleaning, or sleeping. She had studied his anatomy. He was heavy in the haunches, but his face was thin and pointed. His almost black toes showed sharp white claws peeking out. His thin legs spread into the beige body with grace, strong and agile. The cat wore a sky blue satin ribbon that accented the color of his eyes. Anne had taken note of the light shining on his ears and the black tail that wrapped so closely around his body like a thin snake with its tip raised ready to register any movement of which he should be aware.

The Siamese breed had the distinguishing dark muzzle and ears. Edward's paws were covered with the darkest fur; a camouflage for in the forest perhaps, to hide their legs from being seen by predators, snakes and rodents. The short silky fur on the rest of Edward's body started out almost white at the shoulders and hips, but was a brown by the time the fur reached the center of the feline's back. Again Anne imagined how the shading of his coat did well to hide the cat in the speckled light of shrubbery where his quarry might be found.

Three other features marked Edward as a Siamese; his crooked tail, his crossed eyes, and his obvious show of superiority. Edward was regal and expected to be treated as such. For now, he would allow Anne to make her drawing.

When Miss Moser saw the sketch the following morning, she was pleased to the edge of tears.

"Oh, my Edward! Oh Anne, how wonderful. He has never had his portrait done. It will be a challenge, if your subject does not return to sit for you," she teased. "I see you are drawing with a feeling for later shading. You will enjoy the freedom and the vast options oils are going to give you for your project."

"I believe he knows I am doing a study of him, and he is pleased," Anne teased back.

The following day, Anne finished her sketch. It had not been more than minutes before the cat arrived to sit on the same sofa in the same spot; his body positioned just a quarter turn off from where it had been the day before. Anne had sketched enough to begin to paint.

Miss Moser opened her box of paints. She drew out several bottles of pre-mixed paints. Millie came forward with an oval palette on which Anne could test and mix her colors. Once again the box of bristle brushes was brought to the matron and she chose several for Anne to use.

"These brushes with the red hairs are not of the quality of the bristles in this white brush. It is made from a Russian hog that is known to hold its shape against the roughest of treatment. The others are fine for moving color about, but when definition is required, perhaps for Edward's fur, you will want to make use of this finer brush. She placed the brushes in the slanted tray of oil in the middle of a circle of paints, and then sat back in her chair.

"Anne, I want you to tell me all the colors you see when you look at Edward."

"I see brown, of course, white for his whiskers, the tips of his ears, and the edge of his thigh where the light hits it. I see black along his nose and the tip of his paw that is poking out from under his chest. There is light blue where the light from the window is the strongest, and I see almost a sea color down his back.

"Anne, you are a treasure," Miss Moser said, gripping her own hands together in a hand shake in front of her.

Anne could tell she had answered well by the lady's expression, but she had not thought twice about the answer. That is what she saw.

"You are ready to paint, my dear," the elderly artist said, reassuringly. "There are these colors and more as you saw. Take up the palette and a bit of a few colors you think you might use to make your farthest away point. You want to paint from the back forward, and from light to dark or dark to light, building layers as the form and colors come in focus. The last strokes of the brush will either be white or black more times than not. They are the two borders to the realm of colors." The elderly artist took a breath. She was so excited to be sharing this new world with so capable an explorer.

"If you would like, you can practice some strokes on another canvas, but I practice as I paint, covering my experiments with the painting. As the layers come forth, it will be necessary to use more oil to move the tints about. You will want to paint the floor beyond the sofa and table grey or brown, or you can paint the entire background behind the cat one color and then build from there." Miss Moser pointed to the area as she explained her thoughts to Anne.

"The Dutch style that I fell in love with tends to start with a dark background color. I loved a dark blue, for instance. Rembrandt used a charcoal black and came forward with lighter colors as he defined his subject, thus, the muted, darker look to his paintings. With such a cheery view, the brightness from the window, and the daffodils in the vase, you may wish to start with a lighter color. It is not necessary to copy what you see here exactly, any muted background will do." She did not want to overwhelm

Anne, but she had so many other tips she had yet to share. Anne's ability had moved the lessons forward so quickly.

"I am anxious for you to feel free with the paint. I am not going to disturb you until you are ready to add a second layer and begin to add details. Have fun with the paints and see how easily they change for you. You will have much more control than you did with watercolors. The rags hanging from the back of the easel will clean any paint from your hands and also from the brush between colors. A clean rag can be used to remove paint from your canvas if you feel your color choice is wrong or you have been too eager with your addition of oil. It is more difficult to remove from clothing, so take care to wear your apron always. Any questions?"

Anne shook her head and looked up long enough to see the lady take a seat at the other side of the room and begin to write a note. Anne reached for her first bottle, taking the paint out with one of the red haired brushes. She saw that is was the dull brown called Umber. Next to it was the Sienna, a redder brown. She was familiar with these names as they were the same in watercolors. She saw there was another brown, Sepia, waiting on the table, so she took a bit of it out also. It was an even darker brown. With the addition of white and even a little green, Anne created the color she wanted for the background beyond the sofa. Painting those areas, she realized that unlike watercolors, these fixed paints would not move outside the brush stokes she made. To add more paint and brighten the color as the view came forward, it was necessary to add more oil. Soon, she began to have more control of the dispersal of the paint and decided to work on the small couch where the cat still slept.

The color Anne created with the brown and white paints did not reflect the off white of the sofa correctly, so Anne dragged a bit of the yellow paint with her brush from the pile she had placed on her palette. The soft buttery color was perfect for the back and the cushions. As she painted out to the edges of the seat and the top of the back where the light hit, she added more white to the paint she had mixed. This worked so well that Anne played with the color, moving it out to the arm of the sofa and then mixing the color back darker again to indicate the shadow of the inner arm of the sofa down to the darker beige area directly above the cat's back.

As she began the shape of Edward's back against the sofa, she added the sea green color she saw there. The colors merged perfectly in a way watercolors never did. She continued to define the cat's shape with the brush until it was completely dry of paint. A hair from the tip came off and she worried she had damaged the brush in her enthusiasm. She captured the hair with her fingernail, but did not say anything of it to her teacher, remembering she had mentioned the lower quality of the brush.

One last swipe of the beige color she had mixed for the couch used what was left on the palette. She kept adding more brown paint as she came around the shape of the cat's back. Then she added a bit of black as she began the stripe that would eventually be the cat's thin dark brown tail.

Wiping the color from the brush as Miss Moser had indicated, she returned the brush to the oil. She chose the white haired brush and returned to working on the cat's shoulders where his fur spread from beige to almost white, reflecting the outdoor light. As she added strokes for his neck and then towards his face, the area assumed its feline shape. Anne could imagine all the parts that she had not painted, seeing the dark ears and muzzle, the blue eyes, and the white whiskers. Little by little she closed in on these details with the remaining pile of beige paint she had created and a new dark brown she mixed with sepia and a black called Vine Black.

She was concentrating so closely on her work that she forgot Miss Moser sitting at the other end of the room until she stood. "I think it is time for a bite to eat. Can you pull yourself away?" The lady asked.

Anne knew she understood her excitement. "I suppose," she said, smiling at the elderly woman. As she stood, her neck ached as she straightened it. She was surprised how tense she was from concentration. She rolled her shoulders and placed her head on each shoulder to relieve the ache in her neck.

"You are doing so well experimenting with the paint. I am so proud of you for trying something new with such willingness. Nothing in nature is quite the color it appears without it being made of many colors altogether. Even a cat's back." She bent down to run her wrinkled hand across Edwards back. He responded immediately with a squinty look of love and a purr. "He sits as if he knows you are painting him!" She smiled at her student with pure delight.

"Oh, you are on to the details of his face. Very well. You have done fine to this point. I will not say a word until you ask for help. The black you have chosen, is a favorite of mine. The name "Vine Black" is derived from the fact it is burnt grape vines that give the color. It tones down bright colors," she said as she continued to stroke the purring cat.

"I think he likes me constantly looking over at him. He only stood and stretched once, repositioning himself a quarter turn, but with the light hitting him at the same angle. He sits well for his portrait." Anne giggled and took her mentor's arm leading her out to the hall.

As they sat down to lunch, Miss Moser once again asked if Anne had any questions about the new method she was using. "I do wonder about all the browns," she had the chance to say. "They have Italian sounding names; Sepia and Sienna for instance."

Miss Moser smiled. "The name Sienna is indeed Italian as indicates the location of the mine from which the pigment comes. Umber is also named for Umbria the location in Southern Tuscany where the umber clay is dug. Sepia, however, is the term associated with the ink dye that a cuttlefish, similar to an octopus, squirts into the water to escape predators."

"Oh my," was all Anne could say, wondering how it was ever discovered to be useful for painting.

MISS *Moser's Student*

"At the end of the week, we will go to The Gardens at Kew to paint; "plein aire" as it is called. We can choose any number of subjects. A morning outside will be good for both of us." Miss Moser announced.

She knew the young woman had been cooped up in the house for quite awhile. First it was her clothes that limited her moving out and about in town, then it was her manners. Though she had grace enough, Miss Moser was quietly teaching her the way things were done. Tea time, their meals together, even the discussions they had were lessons.

Anne had learned by mimicking her whole life. She was quick to observe the elderly matron's mannerisms and copy them. Miss Moser observed that Anne was ready to go out as her companion as well as her student. She would enjoy exposing the pretty girl to new experiences.

Anne was pleased to hear of the outing. She would love to paint outdoors, but even to walk and breath fresh air excited her. She drank the last bit of her tea with a larger than acceptable gulp, anxious to get back to her painting of Edward. Miss Moser excused her, happy to remember her own enthusiasm from long ago.

Once each morning and afternoon, Anne noticed Millie would come into the studio quietly to watch over her shoulder. Minutes later she would have slipped out again unnoticed. When Miss Moser gave instruction, Millie seemed to pay keen attention. As Anne worked on Edward's whiskers, Millie came into observe.

"Do you draw, Millie?" Anne asked.

"In the evening, sometimes," Millie said, a little shy in her admission.

"I would love to see, if you would let me," Anne said.

Millie just smiled and left the room shortly thereafter. When she returned a little later she had two papers in her hand. Anne looked up and put down her brush to take a look.

"Oh, it is me!" She exclaimed. It was the view the maid had while standing at the back work table. Millie had drawn Anne's back sitting at the desk painting with the window beyond. The lines were timid, much like Anne's own first drawings, but the angle of the picture was unique, and the representation was, all in all, well done. The second drawing was small. It was a still life of Miss Moser's dressing table top. The items were very realistic in Millie's representation. No doubt the maid had arranged the brush, mirror, tubs of creams, and perfume bottles every day since her arrival here. The image would be imprinted in her mind's eye. Millie had even included a bit of the reflection in the mistress' mirror, adding to the dimension of the sketch.

"Oh, I really like this one," Anne said. She turned over the scrap of paper and saw several stripes of watercolor. Anne realized Millie had used discarded paper.

"Do you have any paints to add some color to these?" Anne asked.

"No, but I think of purchasing a set one day," the maid answered.

"I have a set in my trunk I would very much like to give to you. Here, take a sheet of this paper for your next drawing."

Millie reached out timidly. "Do you think it is alright?"

"I think Miss Moser would have no objection to my letting you have a piece of paper. Have you shown her your artwork?"

"Oh no, Miss. I would not wish to bother her."

"Millie, I am proof enough that Miss Moser believes even a housemaid can be an artist!" Anne smiled brightly at Millie as she returned her drawings. She would find her supplies and give them to the maid. A perfect use for her abandoned paint set and paper.

10

*T*he day of the outing arrived to a bright sun that emerged early from the fog. It was still chilly, but Anne was pleased to see the trip would not be forestalled by rain. As they drove through the streets of the city, many people were out walking as the weather permitted. Crossing the river, Anne looked out to see barges and sail boats moored along the edges. They passed a guard house where the uniformed soldier cleared them to enter and the carriage proceeded through an iron gate to finally stop between a large, stately house and an even larger tree-lined park.

Descending from the carriage, Anne saw that the expanse of the park started as a lawn area behind the house which faced the river beyond. As Anne followed along behind Miss Moser and the footman, she paused on the path gazing at the views which the mistress had forecast.

"I think you will find many ideas for paintings when spring arrives and the flowers begin to bloom. The snowdrops will be out and the cyclamens soon, so I like to go now to appreciate each flower as it arrives," the matron said.

Indeed, Anne could see so many possibilities for painting, even if most of the flowers were not yet in bloom. The snow from the week before was gone. Another storm was due in the following days, but for now, the sky was clear and except for the cold breeze, the brightness promised a good afternoon for painting.

The artists had dressed for the occasion. Anne was wrapped in a heavy wool cloak Miss Moser had pulled from her closet. She had tied her new bonnet as tightly under her chin as she dared, not wishing to damage the satin ribbon. The brim caught the wind like a sail, curling it back and steering her a bit off course as she followed the matron on the gravel path. Anne's cheeks stung as the cold wind swept across the open park. She could barely feel her nose, but the early Spring sun and the chance to be outdoors in such a lovely setting made her forget her discomfort quickly.

As they entered the large opening, Anne heard voices coming from the far end. She could see several young men playing cricket with shouts and whoops that boomed across the lawn. Their vests abandoned and their untied neck cloths slapping, they ran back and forth for their game. She guessed these could be the princes and perhaps some of their friends. The knowledge made her feel very small. She trotted to catch up with Miss Moser. The footman followed behind wheeling the cart with easels and painting supplies.

"I want you to see the Queen's cottage. We will not bother anyone, as I believe she is elsewhere. The view is beautiful now and come early summer when the bluebells bloom, the view will be extraordinary. We come for pleasure only, so sketch whatever makes you most happy." She smiled back to Anne. She had meant to comment sooner, but the young woman's eyes had been on the cricket players. Some eyes from that end of the lawn had been looking back at her. How fun to be an onlooker, Miss Moser mused.

MISS *Moser's Student*

The boy with the bat missed the pitch, and groans came from the rest of the boys.

"Oh God, Willie," the boy pitching the ball said to the other with the bat, seeing that the batter's attention was on the group making their way across the far end of the lawn. "A female comes within a mile and like a wolf, he begins to hunt her," he remarked to the other boys. "Are you going to play or not?" The pitcher asked.

"Who is the old woman?" the batter asked, ignoring his friend's inquiry.

"The Moser woman. She comes to paint flowers. A little old for you though, my boy."

"Who is the girl?"

"Ah, I have never seen her before. The old woman usually is accompanied by a footman and a maid. The maid is a scrawny thing, nothing to look at. I would have remembered this one." The batter missed another pitch on purpose and grabbed the ball instead, to go out. Once again there were groans. He walked past the bowler, passing him the ball and headed toward the two artists now set up on the path to the Queen's cottage.

"Where are you going, Will?" the pitcher asked.

"I have seen her before." He turned and sneered wickedly, lifting his eyebrows in a devilish expression.

"We will lose the wager if you do not return quickly," the young man holding the ball complained.

There was not one of the men assembled for their game that was not in awe of the player who was walking away. He was the nephew of the Duke and would claim a title of his own one day. They were not impressed by this as most of them would hold a title of some sort in their future. It was their friend's unabashed manner that intrigued them. None of them could brag to be as rude or as heartless a rake as this fellow nobleman. He held their attention if not their respect.

Miss Moser chose the edge of a wooded area for their point of view. From there, they could see the Queen's cottage. Anne was amused to think such a humble dwelling had been built at the wishes of a person who could also afford a castle. Perhaps that was the point, she mused. Would the Queen have enjoyed the ancient cottage in which Anne had lived with her father on Lord Greville's estate? She thought not as she remembered the milky windows and the cold stone floor with a smile.

Anne chose not to work at the easel. She wanted to carry her paper closer to a cobnut bush she spotted along the edge of the large oaks. She wanted to draw the catkins, buds, and tiny red flowers that bloomed for only a few days this time of year. She began her sketch, thinking of so many mornings in Lord Greville's greenhouse. They had all started in this very same way.

Anne startled when she heard a man address Miss Moser. The surprise came not only from his proximity, but also with alarm at the familiarity. She cringed when she heard that voice. She kept her eyes down on her paper and pretended to be sketching. She retraced the lines she had already drawn, pressing into the paper to prevent her hand from shaking.

"And this is your student, My Lady?" The boy was asking.

"Yes," Miss Moser replied, urged on by the boy's pleasant manner, aware that he had been one of the cricket players and no doubt of noble birth.

"Ah, she is drawing the common cobnut, how quaint," he said with some degree of condescension, "and appropriate," he added disparagingly.

Just as Anne feared, it was definitely the Duke's nephew. He came closer until he stood directly behind her. She had been in this very position the day she defied him, and he had cruelly pulled a lock of hair from her scalp.

MISS *Moser's Student*

"So nice to see you, Anne," the boy whispered for her ears only.

Anne's skin crawled. She could not control the icy shiver that caused a spasm of terror up her back to the base of her neck. Her body was frozen with fear and heavy with hatred. She wished she could turn and spit in his face. He would not dare harm her in plain view of her companions.

Miss Moser did not know what the young man's intentions were, and despite his familiarity with the princes, she did not like the way the boy had approached Anne so quickly. The elderly woman heard the tone of voice he used with his young friend. She was not altogether unfamiliar with the ways of such boys and men. It was her turn to protect Anne.

"As my student has only a short time for the light to be just so, I beg your pardon if I ask that we be allowed to continue the lesson uninterrupted."

Anne turned to give Miss Moser a look of appreciation while the young nobleman gave a mediocre bow, "Your servant, Ma'am." He took off at a steady clip across the lawn.

"I hope to see you again soon, Anne," he taunted as he called back over his shoulder.

Miss Moser was shocked. The two knew each other? She would not have guessed as much during the visit. Yet, surely he had called her name. She debated if she should ask Anne about the young man, but remembering the girl's sadness whenever asked about her past, she thought better of it. They would enjoy the day unencumbered, or so she thought. When she looked over at Anne, she reconsidered.

The young woman was facing the hazelnut, but Miss Moser could see her shoulders were shaking with silent sobs.

"What is it, my dear? You know that boy? Do not let him concern you. We are here to draw. Put him and all that happened before away for now. Use your art and ability to make beauty where before it did not exist."

Anne listened to the woman's words, and thought to herself how wise she was. Yes! She must not allow Lord William to hurt her. Every tear she shed was a joy to him. His cruelty could only be daunted by her strength to ignore him. He must never see her cry. She moved her sketch to the easel, resolved to finish as she addressed Miss Moser's questions.

"That is the Duke's nephew. He is the reason I was sent to stay with my father." She steadied her voice as looked over the matron's shoulders in the direction the nobleman had headed.

Miss Moser was pleased that Anne would explain; that she trusted her enough to share her pain's source. "You loved him?" she asked misunderstanding.

"No, he is heartless. He took advantage of me. I was caught in a compromising position. I was innocent, but they sent me away, all the same." Anne fought back tears, thinking of her previous home. Lord William had caused her to be separated so callously.

"Yes, that is how Society tends to deal with such things. Those of lower stations often take the blame for mistakes. I imagine they could not leave such a pretty temptation before the boy." Miss Moser leaned over and patted Anne's arm.

It was a simple gesture, but so reassuring. Anne wondered if she had found a friend in this elderly artist, though such a prospect frightened her. She had felt that way about Lord Greville, and yet catastrophe had severed that bond shortly thereafter.

"For months I have grieved about that event, but now, as you say, I must reason with my past as it has led me to my present. For the first time, I am glad I was sent away." Anne felt a burden had been lifted. Miss Moser's words had given her the strength to reconsider how things had turned out. "I fear he is not finished with me though. He will find some way for retribution. That is his way," she said darkly.

MISS *Moser's Student*

Miss Moser considered Anne's words, worried at their assurance. She felt a motherly instinct toward Anne and would be on her guard against the young man. Inquiries could be made.

The sun was traveling below the tops of the trees that edged the garden. She summoned the footman to pack up their things as the wind was increasing and the temperature dropped. Miss Moser asked him to check if the men were still playing on the lawn. The footman reported there was no one about.

Anne carried her head high as she crossed the opening where the boys had spotted her. She would not let them see any effect Lord William may have caused to her nerves. He could only hurt her if she let him, she kept reminding herself. She was no longer the Duke's nursery maid. She was Miss Moser's student.

When they returned home, Miss Moser invited Anne to her room for a late cup of tea and supper. Anne was happy not to eat a dinner alone. When she entered the lady's room, she was busy at her wash basin dousing her eyes. As Millie passed her a towel, she saw the pain on Miss Moser's face. Instinctively, she went to her.

"Do your eyes her hurt so much?" Anne asked.

"They are sore and dry from the cold air, but it is the wash that stings."

"Anne took up the bottle she had retrieved from the apothecary. She would not visit the memory of those blue eyes now. She smelled the infusion and then asked, "May I?" She indicated she wished to pour a bit on her finger to taste. Miss Moser thought it unusual, but consented.

Anne could taste the bitterness of strong herbs in the concoction, but not a hint of what she was hoping for. She thought whether or not she should resolve the lack immediately, but thought better of it for the mistress' sake. She would go to the apothecary shop in the morning if Miss Moser allowed.

11

nne envisioned finding the young shop keeper waiting at his counter as she swung open the front door of the apothecary shop. She never heard the jingle of the bell because she was so ready to do battle. She had thought of several clever things to say to the handsome helper. Instead, a much older man stood in his place. Anne was put off guard. She had so wished to retaliate for the young man's rudeness. As she closed the door, she saw the object of her derision restocking bottles in the corner behind the door. He looked up, ceased his work, and made his way to the counter to stand next to the other man.

The younger man thought the woman's face familiar, but he did not immediately come to recall Anne and her previous visit. This lady was very pretty, that much he knew.

"Might I help you, Miss?" her intended mark asked. The other man smiled at Anne and left for the back room as if he had been directed to do so.

"Yes, I picked up some eye wash for Miss Moser a few weeks past, and I am curious to know what ingredients you include in the recipe.

Now he remembered, John said to himself. This was the maid he'd thought so pretty last time, just before she had lashed out at him. She had not appeared as well dressed as she did now. Where she had worn an old loose cloak, she now wore an attractive, well-fitted pelisse that followed the contours of her slim body exactly. Her hair was pulled back under a bonnet, but a curl had escaped along the side of her face. He had not noticed the blush to her cheeks, but he did remember those dark eyes. He realized she was asking him a question.

"Excuse me?" he asked awkwardly.

His manner had not changed, she noticed. His boorish demeanor of addressing her with disregard continued. "I wish to know what is included in the eyewash the apothecary prepared for Miss Moser," Anne repeated. She tried pronouncing her words without his knowledge of her provocation. She would not give the man any merit for his behavior. She would not be put in her place.

John Parker heard her this time and her tone. He answered with a starch, "I prepared the wash." It was not his custom to share the ingredients with a customer. As men of medicine, apothecaries did reveal their mixtures and their successes with their colleagues contrary to the practice of quacks. The unskilled sold their miracle ointments and concoctions while intentionally hiding the contents which often included dubious ingredients. As a member of the elite Society of Apothecaries, John did not relish this line of questioning and the young woman's scrutiny. He took his profession seriously. After all, the recommendation of certain medicines could conceivably save life or cause death.

"Is there eyebright?" Anne asked, undaunted by his pause and attempt at superiority.

"Yes, of course," the man answered, annoyed he answered the pretty young woman despite his inner qualm. He was surprised that once again she had infuriated him.

"And rue? She asked.

"Yes" was all he would say.

"Did you add fennel? I did not smell the herb."

"No, I do not use fennel. I added a bit of borage." He could not believe he continued to divulge the ingredients.

"You do not add salt?" Anne asked.

"No, I do not." John Parker looked into the woman's face. No, he did not add salt. What of it? Who was she to be questioning him? Though in the past, some apothecaries had been abused, the trend in Society now held them in high regard. Working alongside physicians, apothecaries had become quite respected.

"If you do add a bit of salt, it makes a red, sore eye sting less. The slight taste of salt in the wash soothes the burn the other herbs may cause." She said it with a "don't you know" finality which was not missed by the young doctor.

"Are you so familiar with these things, Miss? Are you not an art student?" He threw back at her sarcastically. It was the tale she had spun on her last visit. She had been dressed so plainly that day, and yet now he might believe she was studying with Miss Moser as she had mentioned. He listened as she explained. He saw her address him with an upturned face and a great deal of pride.

"I have drawn many of these plants. My mother was well versed in the use of herbs," she said, though her mother's knowledge was more instinctual rather than scholarly. "I learned from her."

"And I have studied at the university to gain my knowledge of the use of plants. I am not accustomed to housemaids questioning my medicines. Miss Moser has been a customer for several years, and I have yet to hear her complain." He realized his words carried a bitter tone, not the best to use with a client.

"And you will not. I only suggested you make an addition of salt. You may try it yourself and see. I wish only the best for your patients." Anne turned to leave.

"I am sorry if I offended you." He called behind her. He did not wish to send the woman off to Miss Moser with any ill will. His father would not appreciate losing as good a customer as Miss Moser.

Anne knew her appearance had much to do with the young man's reactions. Would he have apologized if she wore her old coat? She was a new person. She felt more worthy. Her rude demeanor was equally new to her. "You have not offended me. I am only wishing to help, but what do I know? I am only a "housemaid" after all." She would leave him with that remark and headed for the door.

Before she could reach it, he caught up to turn the handle for her. He stood only inches away. Looking into her eyes with the best smile he could under the circumstances, he wondered how she could raise his ire so quickly.

Anne was determined not to fall victim to his beguiling smile. The depth of his light blue eyes would not trap her. Anne preferred not to like him and would not overlook his arrogance because of his handsome face. She had fallen for Tom in such a way; making excuses for what she knew were faults.

"Please tell the apothecary that Miss Moser will call for a consultation next week."

John kept his anger in check as she continued to ignore his credentials. Instead he replied nicely, "I look forward to it."

MISS *Moser's Student*

Anne gave him a look that was meant for all the scheming men she had known. He stood to the side, allowing her to pass. The scent of roses wafted behind her, rising above the spices inside the store and the smell of soot outside. He watched her rejoin a maid and continue down the street without exchanging a word.

When John turned back around, his father was waiting at the counter with a jovial smile."You were quick to aid the pretty girl," his father chortled.

"Yes, but no need to get excited, she is quite angry at me for some reason and wishes to challenge my knowledge of my chosen profession."

"Yes, but she has your interest now. Something no other woman has yet to achieve," his father said.

"Well, don't tell mother or she will have us marrying in a month's time. The girl is not to be wooed, whoever she is; a lovely to look at creature with a venomous temperament."

"I thought she said she was Miss Moser's student," his father said.

"Yes, well, even that does not seem clear."

James Parker merely smiled, lit his pipe, and returned from the store front to his mixing in the back room. John returned to his replenishing, pushing too many jars on the shelf until they began to fall and he had to catch two. He was flustered by the girl's utterly aggravating manner, and yet curious about her recommendation. When he finished, he stepped back to speak to his father, his mentor in the business. "Have you ever added salt to any of the eye washes, Father?"

"I have heard of it and it does make some sense that the tears are salty and the eye might react favorably to the salt, but it will not aid in the dispensing of the medicine, so I have never done so."

"If it made the wash sting less, would it be a reasonable addition?" The younger apothecary asked.

"I suppose, though it could change the compounding herbs to sit in salt water for an extended period of time. Perhaps that is why it is not used more often.

"If the wash were used frequently, and not left to ferment, could it be a helpful addition?" The younger man asked again.

"You can try it, I suppose, and answer your own question. Why do you ask?"

The son was embarrassed to bring up the recommendations of the young woman. He would not give her the credit immediately.

"Oh, the thought came to me. As you said, I must try a bit myself and see."

12

*T*he watercolor show was one of the first events of the Season at Vauxhall. The weather had permitted opening the gardens early, and most everyone was anxious to get out and be seen. As a public garden, it was a good place for those on the cusp of good society to mingle in the company of the upper crust, the ton, the people everyone wanted to be.

Miss Moser thought it would amuse Anne to attend. They had been out to town so little, and Anne deserved some diversion from her quiet household. She wanted the young woman to see that some of the works she was producing were of the caliber of the artists displaying their artwork this year. Vauxhall would be lovely now, new and fresh, not stale and used as the park would appear later in the year when night after night of frivolity took its toll.

Attending the show would offer Anne an opportunity to meet other artists; at least that was part of the elderly artist's intention. Somewhere at the very back of her thoughts was the notion that Lord Greville might attend. She felt Anne needed to see the nobleman. Sir Joseph had inquired as to the status of "her promising new student" in a missive about a Royal Academy membership. Miss Moser had replied how happy she was to have taken Anne under instruction; how rewarding the relationship with the young woman had proven to be. As of yet, she had never been in communication with Lord Greville, and that held questions for her.

The show was displayed in the rotunda and in two smaller galleries. In addition, some artists had set up displays along the Grand Walk. Miss Moser toured the large area of the show in the round building her father had helped to build. Anne and several other visitors remarked on favorites, techniques, and they shared information about the artists. Anne had spoken to two other young women of a similar age, and the conversation seemed to flow naturally. By the end of the rotunda, Miss Moser's eyes ached, and her neck was stiff from craning. The elderly artist found an unoccupied table and took a seat to rest.

"You go on with the others. I am going to sit here for a bit."

Anne proceeded back out into the flow of visitors, excited to continue with the same small group of which she had become a member. She felt distinguished in her new walking dress, jacket, and satin slippers. Miss Moser had warned her to stay on the paths lest her new shoes become water-stained.

The group of young people made their way through the next gallery. Anne was surprised to see so many different interpretations. Some of the more impressionistic school did not attract her eye as much as the paintings in the realism style. She hoped with practice and continued guidance from Miss Moser that she could produce something of the sort presented here.

At the end of the display in the second garden, Anne thought to walk back to where Miss Moser rested, but the group continued and Anne was swept along with them until she was able to get to the side of the walkway where the current of people was not as strong. As there was an intersection to her side, she stepped into the opening to wait for a break in the mass of bodies coming toward her.

She felt a tug at the elbow of her jacket, but before she could react, someone grabbed her arm and pulled her back into the garden behind a tall hedge. When she could finally get her balance and turn, the face of Lord William met her, lit with a sinister grin. She stiffened immediately.

"Ah, Anne, we meet again," he said, pulling her down the path. She started to fight him, trying to break free from his hold on her wrist. There was no one walking through the garden at this end. He took her other wrist together with the one he gripped so tightly. He twisted them behind her back as his body bounced against her, pushing her along.

"If you cause a scene, I will say I do not know who you are. I will say you brazenly approached me. It will not bode well for you as a nobody to have set upon one who is so well connected."

She thought of all the times at the abbey when he intimidated everyone around him.

He berated maids and footmen alike. He woke babies in the nursery. He teased little ones by taking their toys. He would lead the younger children into trouble and then disappear when the punishment was handed out. She had feared him. She had reviled him, but she had been powerless. She was a nursery maid and a gardener's daughter.

William kept tightening his grip on Anne's wrists, pushing her further from the crowd. She feared if they crossed the next row of trees, they would be absolutely alone, and he would be able to do as he wished with her. She was truly frightened.

When the pocket of her coat snagged on a bush, Anne watched the seam tear before coming free from the branch. He pushed her off the path and her thought went to her new shoes. She could scream, she hated the nobleman so much, but she knew what he said was true. He could make her out as the poor girl bothering the nobleman. She had been blamed for his antics before.

Lord Greville entered the throng of Vauxhall visitors at the elaborate front gate. He paid his three shillings and walked to the first gallery where the watercolor paintings were displayed. He was about to enter when he recognized Mary Moser sitting alone at a table across the patio.

Fortune had been kind to him. He had hoped he might sometime meet the elderly artist by circumstance. He would ask off-handedly about Anne, and the aching curiosity that nagged at him would at last be satisfied. He did not deliberate long before proceeding across the opening to speak with her. Familiar with her near-sightedness, he bowed low and spoke softly, "Miss Moser?" He asked, seeing he had her attention. "I am glad to reacquaint myself to you. Charles Francis Greville," he stated.

"Oh yes, Lord Greville. Won't you have a seat?" She said slowly. She looked the gentleman in the eyes as he sat across from her. She saw the expression she had seen on Anne's face so many times. It was a look of bridled constraint. A heart's desire reined in. She knew the look and the pain it caused. She had loved a married man once. "I wish to speak to you," she said.

Charles was pleased, as he wished to speak to the lady, as well. His curiosity about Anne was like a pin prick to his heart that he could not soothe. He thought of the young artist daily, worrying about how her life had progressed after he had sent her off; a life of which he missed being a part. So many things reminded him of her. He recalled their meetings with pleasure, more than many other events in his life.

"I was-," they each began.

"Oh, so sorry, Ma'am," the lord said.

"That is quite alright. I suspect we are wishing to speak on the same subject."

The lady's smile informed him that perhaps she was correct.

"Miss Blake, Anne, has continued down the walk to see the displays," the lady pointed across the patio. "I was tired and sought this table. I expected her back by now," the lady added. She wished for Anne to reunite with Lord Greville. She hoped to heal their differences. She mentioned briefly how pleased she was with the arrangement. She remarked on Anne's skill as an artist, and thanked Lord Greville for his consideration. She wished she could glean more information about their relationship, but it would be awkward to direct the conversation to the subject.

"She is straight ahead, you believe?" the lord asked. "I could fetch her."

"I would appreciate it. She has little experience with this sort of affair. There are the usual rakes and scoundrels about. I suppose I should have not left her with the others.

Would you be so kind as to rescue her?" Miss Moser quipped, with no idea it might be necessary.

The nobleman began to head in the direction Miss Moser had indicated, but realized spotting the young woman in the throng might be difficult. "Excuse me, but what color might she be wearing?" he asked.

"Look for a pale blue coat. She is wearing a straw bonnet. Her hair is pulled up in the front, but still loose in the back.

Lord Greville would know her hair anywhere. He had held a lock of it once. The pale blue coat would make her easier to find in the crowd. He made his way quickly through the first display until he was once again on the Grand Walk. He did not see Anne anywhere ahead and thought to search in the alcoves. He worried he would not find her before she returned to Miss Moser. That would prevent having a private word with her.

He caught a glimpse of silver blue shining through the grove of trees across the orchard on his left. He carefully ducked through the trees to get a better view. When he stood up, he saw the unmistakable waves of dark brown hair cascading down the woman's back. Anne was being tugged through the trees by an impeccably dressed young man. He appeared to be a young nobleman, but perhaps merely a dandy. Anne did not appear to be willing, though she did not cry out.

As the lord came in direct view of the couple, he saw that Anne was struggling to get away. It appeared that the young man was pulling her to him for a kiss, but Anne fought hard enough to pull free. How odd was the sensation of once again being in the same situation with Anne. Lord Greville lunged at the man, colliding with the couple who were each startled; William for the interruption, Anne for the surprise reunion.

"Unhand her, sir!" Lord Greville announced to the young man.

The boy turned to face the lord, but seeing his age and the cane raised in his right hand, he thought it best to ease the situation.

"The girl will not leave me alone, sir. I am so embarrassed. She comes from such common stock. I cannot be seen with her no matter how much she may desire it."

"I fear you do not know who I am," Lord Greville spoke condescendingly to the much younger nobleman.

"No, sir, I have not had the pleasure," he bowed.

"Indeed, you would not be so mistaken about my niece's behavior if you were aware of who we are. I wonder at the accusations she could now level at you." He looked briefly at Anne, but could not hold his eyes there until he finished.

Lord Greville saw fear come across the young man's face. He did not know Lord Greville, but he could tell he was a man of influence. He could hardly believe Anne was his relative. Had there been some mistake in her serving his family? He thought she had been sent to live with her father, a gardener. This man was no brother to a gardener.

"I apologize, sir. Your servant, Miss." He bowed to Anne and backed away slowly as if avoiding a charging tiger. The expression on his face was no longer threatening.

When Lord Greville looked back at Anne, she was visibly shaken. It might have been a closer call than he first noted. How had she come to get in such a situation again?

"Here I am, saving you from unwanted kisses again." He smiled, quite pleased he had arrived at such a moment in the young lady's life, but then followed it with a true note of concern as Anne pulled her sleeves down over her wrists and examined her torn jacket. "Are you alright? Did he hurt you?"

Anne appreciated Lord Greville's tease. The tone was friendly and familiar. He was kind to try to cheer her up. "Yes. I am alright."

"Who was the young man, a random rake or someone you know? Should I call a guard?" He asked.

Anne looked down. She so hated to explain the man to the lord. "No. He is the Duke's nephew. He is the reason I came to live at your estate with my father so suddenly. He is indeed a rake, but not random. He hates me and I have similar feelings for him. He separated me from the crowd and dragged me across the walkway into these trees where we would not be seen. I am lucky that you arrived." Then shock jolted through her, She shook her head and asked, "How did you come to be here?"

Lord Greville moved closer, feeling her story draw him in. "I spoke with Miss Moser. She was telling me how pleased she was with your progress. She mentioned you had walked on with a group looking at the paintings and had yet to return. I offered to retrieve you."

"I thank you. You saved me from harm, I am sure," Anne said.

"A man does not take so much time with something he detests. The scoundrel may pretend to dislike you, but he sees you as unattainable, something he is attracted to control. Evidently you have put him off before. You have the upper hand with this one whether you desire it or not. Why did you not call out?" he asked.

"As he tried with you, he insisted no one would believe me because of his position in Society."

"No, Miss Blake. Anyone who looks at you would not believe the rogue. You are very much mistaken," he said. She was lovely in her pelisse and bonnet. The intensity had returned to her eyes. The bloom had come back to her cheeks. She looked less sallow and wan. She was a beauty.

It was not as the lord said. She had not put him off when he played his game with her. He had ordered her, and because he had been brutal in the past, she sat in his lap when he demanded. Anne truly wished she had the upper hand with Lord William. She wondered if he had believed the lord's tale.

"Your niece, my lord?" she asked, raising her eyebrows.

"It seemed to work this time, and it may do the trick to keep him away in the future. He fears a bit for his reputation where it matters. If I am someone of influence, he does not want me to make claims against him. Are you ready to return to Miss Moser before she worries when neither of us returns? What do you plan to say to her about this incident?"

"I will tell her what happened when we are away from this place. I do not wish to spoil our visit or have her imagine she was in anyway responsible."

"And you will not wander away again?" he asked.

"No. My party deserted me without a second thought. I suppose Lord William saw me alone. I had not been on the lookout for him as I should have been."

"Surely you cannot look for that man everywhere?"

"It was not our first meeting since I arrived at Miss Moser's." Anne explained. "He saw the mistress and me painting at Kew, one afternoon. I have feared seeing him again since that time, but I was not on guard today."

"Well, he is gone now." The nobleman assured her. He offered her his arm. Anne tucked her arm through his and rested it barely on his sleeve, stiff and self-conscious.

13

ord Greville led Anne out of the orchard by way of a path that ran parallel to the main walk. He allowed Anne to regain her composure, offering his handkerchief which she declined. "I'm fine, thank you," she said. He accepted her smile as a sufficient expression of her ability to once again join the crowd. He was happy the scoundrel was nowhere in sight. He would make inquiries about the boy, but for now, he felt Anne would be safe.

As the nobleman walked her onto the main promenade, he walked with a new pride, pleased to have such a pretty creature on his arm. Passersby nodded and tipped their hats to the couple as they continued through the garden and back to the art displays. Young men kept their eyes on Anne as they paraded by. Would they think she was his mistress, he wondered? His walk became a swagger.

"You are happy with your new position, Miss Blake?" The lord asked, bending closer.

"Yes. Miss Moser is a kind teacher. You have provided me with an excellent opportunity.

"Someday, I hope to repay you for your investment." Anne looked over at the nobleman. She had spent many an afternoon in a closer proximity while they studied flowers, rocks, and stars, but not now. It would not be appropriate for her to be so familiar with the gentleman. She also could not forget he was the one who had given her up.

"My investment? You are only indebted to me to improve your artistic abilities, nothing more."

"I meant the finances you provided for my care," Anne clarified.

"I offered such aid, but Miss Moser declined. She is well provided for by an annuity from her cousin."

Anne was surprised at his answer. She had assumed he had paid to be rid of her. She had not settled her mind on the subject before Lord Greville continued.

"Oh, how the greenhouse has suffered since your father's departure. Danforth failed to keep the heat up on a particularly frosty night. We lost several of the specimens from New Holland. The cold damaged most of the hanging orchids, many of my fuchsias, and all of the plants closest to the doors. I am happy to report that the vanilla survived." His voice held a wink Anne did not see.

Lord Greville had fallen in love with Anne over that orchid. He had been so close to her the day they tried to pollinate the flower. Her sweet rosy smell had been intoxicating. If her father had not burst in and separated them, he was not sure he could have restrained his feelings for her. As it was, he never declared himself. Now here he was arm in arm with the woman. How extraordinary. She was greatly changed. The lord noted that she was no longer the eager and innocent young student, but a subdued and elegant young woman. She made him feel old.

Anne was thinking of her father's diligence, and how lightly he had slept on cold nights. He would check the glasshouse several times if necessary. George Blake had been not only head gardener for Lord Greville, but also an avid horticulturalist in his own right. He would have been disheartened to hear such news.

The lord caught her attention when he mentioned the orchid. Why did the mention of a flower make her heart skip a beat? When she looked over at Lord Greville wondering if he guessed her thoughts, she saw the familiar look of sadness his eyes often reflected. What was not said hung in the air between them. That is how it had always been even after they kissed. So many feelings never allowed to develop, so many words unspoken.

"Mrs. Lambert, she is well? " Anne asked moving away from the familiar ache of longing.

"Yes. Cook and John will be delighted to know you are well. Anne_" he began, wishing he could express all that he felt since he sent her to Miss Moser; how it may have been a mistake.

Loud reports like gun fire interrupted him and they both startled. As a shimmering shower of sparks came down a grove of trees away, they realized a fireworks display had begun. Anne slipped away from the Lord's arm and hurried ahead to join her mentor. Miss Moser waited just as they had left her. She seemed amused, surrounded by loud conversation and laughter. Lord Greville was frustrated. He had lost his chance to speak to Anne; a conversation he had envisioned so many times in the last few months.

"Ah, Lord Greville has found you. Were there many other paintings on the Grand Walk?" She wondered what took Anne so long to return.

"Not so many more, but I did see some landscapes that used sponges as you pointed out." Anne was quick to speak, trying to hide any apprehension she might show. She would avoid telling the lady what had happened unless she was asked. She did not want Miss Moser to feel in anyway responsible.

No one was to blame for Lord William's harassment. He must have seen her confusion as the crowd broke apart at the end of the path. The thought that he had been watching her for a period of time made Anne shiver. She must be more careful in the future.

Miss Moser looked at the couple, but she construed two different emotions from their expressions. Anne seemed aloof and even angry, unseemly for the pleasure garden in which they found themselves. Lord Greville looked caring as if he brought back a lost pet rabbit. What had gone on during their minutes together?

Anne's emotions were so mixed; she could only try to separate them out one by one. Why did it have to be Lord Greville who found her with Lord William? Although she was glad to have been rescued, she would have preferred to meet him under different circumstances. What did he think? Did he believe that she had not solicited these attentions, or did he think she was teasing Lord William as many women chose to do? And what were his feelings in all this? He admitted missing her father for his plant's sake, but what did he feel about seeing her? Was he taken aback in finding her in the man's arms, much like her situation at the dance? Did he feel jealousy? Did he think of her anymore? Anne could make no sense of his feelings. He had tried to speak before the fireworks hindered him. What had he wanted to say?

Lord Greville found he was a little envious of the elderly artist who held Anne's attention and gratitude. No, he had not financed the venture, but he had sought out the position for Anne. He knew if he had insisted, she would have stayed with him on whatever terms he stated. Yet, here she was, beautifully dressed, attracting attention on all sides, and ignoring him to some degree. She half infuriated him. The other half was pure delight and self-satisfaction. He had chosen correctly.

Miss Moser was not sure what to say, or if Anne wanted the meeting with Lord Greville to continue. She could not make out what she should do.

"Anne, do you care to take refreshment or are you ready to depart?"

"I am ready to leave, if you are," she said quickly, feeling anxious about Lord William's whereabouts and discomfited in Lord Greville's presence.

Anne looked back at Lord Greville, aching to tell him she wished to see him another time in another place other than this garden that held such an unpleasant feeling for her now. She was not sure if she could say as much. Instead she said politely, "It was nice to see you again, Lord Greville. Please give my regards to the household." Her heart was sore as she pictured those to whom she sent her regards.

"Yes, certainly. Miss Moser, Miss Blake," he bowed to each of them and was gone.

It was not until Lord Greville moved away that Anne had a view of those sitting around them. Anne admired the woman facing her behind Miss Moser. She was speaking to a man in an eager conversation. She had a look of true admiration on her face as she did so. Her face glowed; the skin was smooth enough to reflect light. Her hair was pulled up into a paisley wrap with a few tresses dangling by her face. The blush on her cheeks indicated one who spent some time out of doors. The woman wore a short gold jacket that accented the colors of her face and hair. Anne thought her a perfect vision; one she might wish to paint.

Anne did not look at the man until he turned his head sideways. It was the clerk from the apothecary shop. He was dressed quite smartly, and she questioned his attendance at the Gardens. Why should the sight of the man give her such a jolt? She turned away from him quickly, hoping he had not seen her with Lord Greville and wondering why.

John Parker had, in fact, seen Lord Greville escorting the young woman across the patio. He was surprised when a seething anger came upon him as he examined the couple. He knew Lord Greville as a friend of his father. Both men shared an interest in geology and mapping England's mineral wealth. Was the rude young woman his mistress? Surely she was too young for the aging nobleman, if there was such a thing in the realm of mistresses.

John Parker was not accustomed to the sensation of caring one way or another. He rarely involved himself with these sorts of things. He seldom held any opinion. As a man of science, he preferred to think beyond the game and intrigue of a relationship with a woman. When he courted his wife, their relationship would run smoothly and honestly as they would both be infinitely sensible people. Theirs would be a match of the most practical sort.

He turned away from the table when he saw that Miss Moser began to rise. Anne had moved around him to help the elderly artist. The apothecary wondered if Anne had seen him. She showed no sign that she had.

The two women left the seating area together. Miss Moser thought it odd that the young apothecary said nothing more to her after Anne's return. The matron had not been able to catch his eye as they departed. He had never looked her way again. They had shared no parting words.

As Anne walked the elderly lady out to the circle where the carriage would pick them up, Miss Moser noticed the seam on Anne's new pelisse was torn. In addition, she spotted the rubbed red marks on Anne's wrists as she reached up to climb into the chaise. Had Lord Greville forced himself on the girl? Was that what she had picked out in their different expressions? Surely not, she reasoned.

With more questions than she could put answers to, Miss Moser settled back for the ride home. When she looked over at Anne who was turned toward the window, seeming to look out, she saw the reflection of Anne's cheeks glistened with tears.

As they reached the house, Miss Moser informed Anne they would have tea in her parlor. Anne wanted nothing more than a quiet moment in her room alone in order to sort through the events of the day. She could not think of a gracious way to avert the invitation. She wondered if the mistress suspected something. Often these teas had some point to them Anne was beginning to realized.

They had settled into their chairs and each had a cup. Miss Moser took a sip and then asked, "Tell me what happened this afternoon."

Anne did not resist her inquiry. The soft, low voice was all-knowing as if she were a wizard. Anne was not altogether surprised her mentor had sensed a change in her mood. Anne wished to choose her words carefully in order to dispel any residual anxiety from showing.

"The Duke's nephew, Lord William, was at the Gardens." She began. "When the group turned at the end of the path, and I became separated from the rest, he grabbed me and twisted my arm. He forced me off the main path. I am not sure what his intentions were. I was afraid to call out as he warned me that others would doubt my word over his. He tried to kiss me, and that is when Lord Greville arrived."

"Oh my word!" Miss Moser exclaimed. "And are you alright?" Miss Moser leaned across the small table and patted the girl's arm. "Let me see your wrists."

Anne pulled back her sleeves reluctantly. She realized Miss Moser must have seen the redness. The skin was bruised and turning a reddish purple where he had gripped her wrists so tightly. The lady went to her dresser and returned with a jar of salve. "Rub this on your arms, dear."

As Anne took a small amount of the green ointment from the container, she thought of the apothecary shop from which the concoction came. Perhaps the clerk had sold it to Miss Moser.

Once again she could feel herself grow tense, just thinking about the man. He, too, had been at the gardens with what appeared to be his girlfriend. Such a strange day.

"What did Lord Greville do about the boy?" Miss Moser wondered if they should have notified the constable. She wished she had known of the incident when they had been at the gardens. Perhaps that was why the girl hid the fact. Anne was not accustomed to having any right to complain, the mistress realized.

"He told Lord William that I was his niece, and that he might be in more trouble than he realized."

Miss Moser let out a laugh. She was glad to see Anne smile, also. "That was quick thinking on the lord's part. And I take it the young man left and was not seen again?"

"Yes, but I was nervous from that point on."

"Of course. No wonder you wished to leave. I thought there had been words between you and Lord Greville and that was your reason for wishing to leave."

"No, though I did not want Lord Greville to find me in such a predicament, I was thankful for his rescue. We shared a short conversation on the way back, but nothing of significance. He mentioned losing some of his plants to the cold, something my father would never have allowed." Anne thought of her short walk back with Lord Greville. She wanted to speak with him on many subjects, but she could not open the barrier that had come between them.

Miss Moser watched the young woman as they both finished their tea in silence. When Anne moved the tray to the table by the door, Miss Moser retrieved a small pink satin box from her dresser. She handed Anne the box and the jar of salve. In here you will find a pair of small assortment of threads and needles, a pair of scissors, and a few pins. Can you manage to repair your sleeve, or would you like Millie to do so for you?"

"Take the salve with you," she added, "I have another jar."

"Yes, thank you. I was so angry when my coat snagged on a branch as Lord William dragged me across the orchard. It did give me the strength to fight back and break his grip."

Miss Moser went to the young woman and embraced her. Anne returned the hug with one of her own. It felt wonderful to be held in such a way.

"You have been so understanding," Anne said. Miss Moser had accepted her with all her complications.

"I will see you for supper, and we will drink a new wine," the artist cheered. "And we will talk about the tea party I have planned for next week. I am inviting my close friends, the Harris's, and I think you will find a new friend or two there."

With that news and thoughts of Lord Greville, Anne headed to the sanctuary of her room where her private thoughts could come to the surface. She shook off the fear and anger at Lord William's attack. She mulled over the conversation with Lord Greville, wishing she had said more. Strangely, though, she felt a little of the pain of the separation from Lord Greville slipped away with today's meeting. When Anne thought of the apothecary's clerk and the beautiful woman accompanying him at Vauxhall, she lied to herself that she did not care.

14

*T*wo days later, Anne was working on some of the finer details of her painting of Edward. An entire morning slipped by as Anne worked on mixing a sky blue she thought appropriate for the cat's eyes and the little bit of blue she could see where the ribbon tucked into the cat's fur around his neck. She applied the color sparingly, uneasy with such a bright addition. She added a little of the blue with some brown to the edge of Edward's arched back where the sun reflected a variety of colors.

She would merge the brown with more beige during her next session in the studio, using the brush made of badger bristles Miss Moser selected for her. "These stiffer hairs are ideal for blending," her teacher had explained. Anne stretched and looked up to realize the morning was almost over. She had thrown herself into her painting after the visit to Vauxhall and her resolve to excel. She was just slipping out the door as Millie came up behind her.

"A package has come for you, Miss," Millie said, handing her a carefully wrapped box tied with several winds of jute string. It was the first package Anne had ever received, and even though it might have been plain, brown paper, and ordinary string, it was exquisitely wrapped in her eyes. She had no idea what it might be or who might have sent it. Lord Greville came to mind. He had given her presents before. The gloves he gave her before the ball had a special place in her bureau even if they might never be worn again.

The package was addressed to "Miss Moser's Student". Millie, Hodges, and now she assumed the package was for her. It was not until she saw the small stamp in the corner that she realized the package came from the Parker Apothecary Shop, the source of Miss Moser's eye wash and the ointment she now had on her wrists. It was also the place of employment of the would-be apothecary with the clear, blue eyes and a talent for angering her.

As she opened the box, a distinct scent of roses came from within. The smell was coming from a lovely glass perfume bottle which had not leaked, but still emitted the scent from the waxed cork. Anne looked at the label to find it was made by the apothecary, John Parker, and gave the address of the shop where she had been twice. Another plain bottle contained eye wash, the same sort she had retrieved her first time at the Parker's shop. Tucked between the bottles was John Parker's card. Anne turned it over to see a message neatly written on the back.

"I am sending you this rose water as a thank you gift. I have added salt to the eye wash and have found that you were correct in saying it eased the extent to which the herbs sting the eyes. I have enclosed a sample for Miss Moser. With my best regards, John Parker, Apothecary."

Anne was confused by the card and signature. She had barely spoken to the apothecary. Her conversation about the addition of salt was with the young store clerk. It was at that moment that she realized the young store clerk was in fact an apothecary in his own right. He must be the older man's son. The revelation came as a shock. Though the young man had mentioned the university, she had been deaf to his claims. He had infuriated her so. And she had called him out on his recipe and been correct. Ha!

And yet, she could not ignore the fact that he had acknowledged her advice. Though she might have preferred an apology for his rude behavior, this gesture could not be slighted. Did he realize she wore rose scent on occasion? She had made her own rose water in the past, but had not done so since last summer at Lord Greville's. She had worn no perfume since the embarrassing night of the dance, but while unpacking her trunk her first day at Miss Moser's, she had rediscovered a bottle. It contained only a little, and she had limited her use. Now, her supply was replenished, and from such an unlikely source.

She wondered at what would be the appropriate action at this point, but decided she would do nothing until she had the chance to thank him in person. She took the bottle of eye wash and walked downstairs for lunch. Though Miss Moser often took her mid-day meal in her own room, she had told Anne she would be eating in the dining hall today, but not tomorrow as she was expecting visitors for an early tea. She said she would speak more of the visit while they were eating together.

Anne entered the room and brought the box with the eyewash to the lady.

"This came today," she said as she put the box at the mistress' place.

"It came to you?" she asked Anne.

"Yes, it was addressed to "Miss Moser's student.""

"Well, that would be you." The elderly woman smiled at the younger woman.

"It appears there was another bottle in the box."

Although she had not asked outright, Anne knew it would be rude to not answer.

"Yes, it was a bottle of rose water, for me." Anne felt so awkward to be sharing in the mistress' package. In the past, a maid would never have received anything in conjunction with a member of the family they served. Not that a servant received packages. Other than Christmas, they very rarely did.

"How nice," Miss Moser said without any haughtiness or demand for further explanation.

Again, the elderly lady had not pried and yet Anne felt she should explain. Why was she reluctant? Was it because she caught herself thinking more of the man's mischievous smile and less of the annoyance she felt when she thought of the young store clerk turned apothecary?

"I suggested the salt addition just as I have been preparing your wash. He tried the wash with and without the salt and agreed that the sting was lessened with the addition. I did not realize he was an apothecary. I had assumed only the older gentleman was the herbalist. I am afraid I argued my case. I am surprised he gave it any credence as I know I angered him as he did me."

Miss Moser continued to smile, thinking of young love and the banters that often occurred. She could see Anne was quizzical about young John Parker, and she was delighted with that knowledge. She remembered how quiet the young apothecary had become when Anne and Lord Greville arrived at her table at the Gardens. Perhaps he, too, had some interest in her pretty protégé.

Anne continued, "So, he sent a kind note and a bottle of rose water in gratitude, I suppose. An apology would have been a nice addition, though we were each rude to the other."

Miss Moser had the maid take the wash to her room. She thought she might send a note of thanks and mention she was proud that her "student" had solved the problem. She best leave it be. No reason to stir these hearts beyond what was already abuzz.

The two women began their meal in silence for a time. When the plates were cleared, Miss Moser began a conversation she had spent some time considering. In the end, she felt she had made the correct decision.

"I am having some dear friends for an early tea tomorrow afternoon, and I wish for you to join us."

Miss Moser had not only been schooling Anne in the mixing of paint and the use of color and shade, but also secretly she had been teaching the young woman social skills. Though Anne arrived from Lord Greville's manor as a polite, well mannered girl, she had not been exposed to some of the finer points of entertaining guests, pouring tea, drinking wine, and dressing appropriately. Without making her intentions obvious, Miss Moser had shared these activities and the like with her student in the hope that Anne might be able to move in higher circles. This would be her first test.

"My friend will be bringing her niece who is studying art, as well. I believe you girls might enjoy one another's company. She is a lovely girl, but quite shy. She does not make friends easily. I felt you might enjoy a visit with someone your own age."

It was a little frightening to be asked to a formal tea with the matron's friends, but she did feel she was ready, and certainly meeting someone her age who was also studying art would be a treat.

"Thank you so much for thinking of me. I should wear my white muslin with the blue ribbon?"

"Yes, that would be appropriate. Do not worry about conversation with Juliette. She may be shy in public forums, but I think one on one with someone her own age, she will not be so."

Anne was far from worrying about shy Juliette as she was about her own ability to enter such an esteemed group. She would do her best to make her mentor proud of the invitation.

"Her brother will join us, as well. He is also here studying. Law, I think. He is a jolly fellow, very American."

15

nne's stomach turned upside down with anticipation as the hour approached for the tea party. The matron had described each guest, and Anne worried if they would truly accept her into their company. This would be her first appearance in the new role Miss Moser was encouraging her to fill. At this tea she would not be just Miss Moser's student, but also her companion.

She wore her new muslin walking dress. Millie had performed a miracle, controlling her unruly hair into a lovely drape of waves at the back of her head that curved onto her shoulders as if breaking on a shore. Still, somewhere inside, Anne could not forget she was a gardener's daughter. She feared the knowledge of that fact would deal her a round of scorn from these visitors. Though they would be a small group, she felt uneasy about what to say. Even worse was her fear that she might be excluded altogether. These fears weighed on her heart more than any qualms about her manners. Miss Moser had been so kind and accepted her so whole-heartedly. It made it imperative for her to gain these people's approval.

Anne poked her head into the drawing room, imagining how it would be an hour from now with the noise of conversation. The high-backed chairs had been pulled into a circle in the middle of the room. At one end of the circle, there was an oval table for the apple-rhubarb cake, muffins and jam, and the small sandwiches that Mrs. Marshall had been preparing all morning. The tea service and six lovely porcelain cups and saucers were lined up in a semi-circle around the tea tray at the other end. One cup would be hers.

Anne was excited to meet two younger members of the party. Henry and Juliette Harris would be attending with their aunt, Benjamin West's wife, Mary, and another mutual friend, Mrs. James Carter, Eleanor, whose husband was the editor of the local paper. The two young adults had been sent to England from America to further their studies and enjoy the connections of their aunt and uncle. Henry was a promising student having received a scholarship in civil law to St. John's College at Oxford, studying law and government. Juliette attended private lessons as she, like her uncle, was a portrait painter.

Miss Moser had remarked that Juliette had skills "beyond her years" and had earned the respect of each of her American teachers who advised her to come to England for further study. Although no women were allowed to study at the Royal Academy, several of the instructors gave lessons elsewhere. Senior students gave lessons as a way to earn extra money. So it was that Juliette continued to hone her skills, while her brother attended college and enjoyed the benefits of a life in England's cultural hub.

Henry also had a passion for boxing, though his aunt did not approve and his mother knew nothing of it. His bouts in the bare knuckled ring had earned him the nickname, Hurling Henry, according to Miss Moser who did not seem shocked or judgmental about Henry's side interest. She said he was able to lift and throw any opponent regardless of his size or weight. When

Miss Moser had told her this, Anne had been even more eager to meet a prize fighter.

For Juliette, Miss Moser had an obvious soft spot of admiration and respect. "When I painted portraits, I felt they never stayed true to their subject. There is something special to Miss Harris' ability to portray the personality of her subject. She is quite gifted in capturing the essence of the person in their expression. Mostly, she has no personal knowledge of the person for whom she is making the portrait, and yet friends and family marvel at the authenticity of her rendering."

Anne was even more excited to meet Miss Harris when Miss Moser went on to say, "As I have mentioned, she is very shy. She has had difficulty moving through society here in London and making new friends." Those words were very reassuring to Anne who definitely was having trouble even imagining moving through society and had to date made no new friends other than the household staff.

When the hour arrived, announced by the hall clock, a knock was heard at the front door. Anne was beside herself with expectation. She stood behind Miss Moser's chair as the guests were announced and shown in by Hodges. As each stopped by the matron's chair and greeted her warmly, she introduced them to Anne. When it was Juliette's turn, she could barely look Anne in the eye. Henry, however, was effusive in his greeting to Miss Moser. His American accent and his burly appearance were immediately endearing. He bowed a bit deeper than he needed and almost lost his neckerchief over his head. Smiling as he came back up, he replaced his cravat and brushed back a bush of brown hair in a casual manner that put Anne at ease. "Please to meet you, Miss Blake."

As the guests were seated and the kitchen maid entered with the hot water and teapot, the ritual of afternoon tea began. Miss Moser took the pot and poured the first cup which she asked Anne to deliver to Mrs. Carter who preferred a weaker cup of tea. Next,

Anne took a cup to Mrs. West, and then Juliette, and lastly Henry before accepting one for herself and sitting at the end of the circle next to Juliette and her brother.

Anne bravely started a conversation, fearful the shy Miss Harris would not.

"Miss Moser tells me you like to paint portraits, Miss Harris."

Henry took a sip of his tea and returned it to his saucer with a clink.

"Please, Miss Blake, may we use first names although we have just met? I tire of the formalities and long to speak to you as I might my friends back home. I am Henry and this is Jules. Your name is Anne, I believe." Anne was surprised by his notion and yet it was a pleasant one. By using their names it would seem they were already familiar with one another and comfortable in that knowledge.

"Certainly, Henry. I am Anne." Anne looked to Juliette to comment. She had appeared fragile as a porcelain doll. Her hair was the color of hay, pulled back in a well behaved bun, nothing like Anne's wild curls. She had pale blue eyes and white skin that showed only a little color on the cheeks. Her top lip formed a perfect bow. She was the closest thing to an angel Anne had ever seen.

"Yes Anne, my name is Juliette, but Jules is so much easier to say. I do enjoy making portraits. My aunt tells me you are a landscape painter and have experience making botanical plates suitable for engraving."

Anne thought of the lost drawings she had made for Lord Greville. She had spent three months making those paintings and had nothing to show for them. "I prefer to paint scenes, but I have painted flowers more than anything."

"Then it is most appropriate for you to be studying with Miss Moser. Her floral displays are so beautiful," Jules replied.

"And Miss Blake, there I go, Anne, how do you like London? I hear you were living at Paddington and in Nottingham before that," Henry inquired, keeping the conversation going.

Anne was startled at a review of her history. What else did these new friends know of her past? "I am becoming accustomed to the hum of the city." She had no anecdotes to exchange. Her outing to Kew Gardens had been marred by Lord William's attendance as had been her only visit to Vauxhall. The episode at the apothecary's had not been altogether pleasant, either, so she really had nothing to say. "Miss Moser has been most kind in showing me the sights of the city," she declared in order to continue the conversation.

"Have you been to Westminster, Anne?" Henry asked.

"We have driven by several times as it so close by, but no, not as of yet." Miss Moser had mentioned they would visit the Abbey and the Justice's Hall, but had not done so.

"Juliette and I will be going soon with my aunt. Perhaps you can accompany us, is that not so, Jules?" Henry stated, including his sister.

"Yes, I have not been inside the cathedral and I have heard it is extraordinary when you are up close. Perhaps, you would like to meet us there, Miss Moser as well?" Juliette entreated.

Miss Moser was watching the conversation at the end of the table, delighted the young people were getting along so well, as she had imagined they might. When she heard her name mentioned at the end of the conversation and saw Anne look her way, she nodded approval. The details of the outing could be sorted later, but for now, she wanted nothing more than for Anne to make new friends.

"I would very much enjoy a visit to the cathedral and taking in the views offered there," she said.

"Yes, and I am not a landscape painter, but we could plan an outing to paint there one day when the weather is nice," Jules added.

"And I will take in the view of any lovely ladies walking about. And food, we must take a picnic," Henry teased.

Anne was so excited to think of a future with these two, new friends who had the same interests as she. The tea continued with more general discussion of the weather, the news of the horrible boating accident on the river, and the mention of an upcoming charity ball, just the reference to which made Anne cringe. She hoped it was not on Miss Moser's list of social obligations she would be asked to attend.

"Anne, Miss Moser called from the end of the table. "Perhaps, Juliette and Henry would like to see what you are working on in the studio."

Initially she felt shy about such a showing, but then assured herself that her new friends were not the type to criticize. Anne led the threesome up the stairs. It was strange to host a visit to the art room, and Anne felt pride in the opportunity to do so. The sister and brother were all compliments as Anne expected they would be.

"What a lovely room in which to paint. So bright!" Juliette stated as they entered.

Henry was silent until he saw Anne's portrait of the cat.

"Ah, Miss Moser's pet. Well done, Anne," he said.

Beaming with delight, Anne returned the couple to their aunt who was in the hall preparing to leave. As they departed they thanked Miss Moser for a lovely afternoon, and each had a kind word for Anne, appreciating meeting her, and showing full praise of her relationship as student and more to Miss Moser.

"I am so pleased Miss Moser has a companion at last. You have brightened her life already, dear. Thank you," Mrs. West said, taking Anne's hand in hers.

MISS *Moser's Student*

Anne could hardly believe her good fortune. Her heart swelled as she relived the afternoon tea and the conversations that flowed around the circle. She thought of Juliette's soft features and equally soft spoken manners and Henry's lack of guile, as her esteem for Miss Moser swelled. It was so kind of her teacher to include her and even possibly have planned the event as an introduction into the artist's society. Anne resolved to work even harder in the studio.

16

The weather continued to be pleasant as storms blew by without delivering much rain. The clouds kept away the fog and warmed the temperatures. Miss Moser planned another outing as she knew the season was progressing and some plants would be in full bloom with the longer days. They would visit the herb garden that ran along the river, the famous apothecary's garden.

Anne had not expected the herb garden to be so full of flowers. She knew there would be a great variety of plants used as medicine, as the Chelsea Physique had been intended to provide. Knowing of plant collections such as Lord Greville's, surely there would be specimens from far off places. She had forgotten, however, that many might be in bloom this late in spring.

Whole masses of purples and yellows beckoned her into the garden. She saw spikes of lavender and the shorter daisy flowers of feverfew along the path as she followed behind Miss Moser and their usual footman, Timothy. They were ready for a fine day of sketching and painting. As they proceeded down a gravel path lined with stone, creeping thyme dotted with light blue flowers extended its vines through the cracks in between the rocks, tickling her shoes. The scent of the herb came up to as they scuffed through, offering a welcoming scent.

Anne stopped to take it all in. It was so beautiful. Her gaze came up from above the plots of herbs to see several other people in the same area as she. They were not milling around, but intent on harvesting sprigs, leaves, and blossoms into baskets. One man was loading larger bundles onto a cart. They were all much busier than she. Anne hurried on to rejoin Miss Moser.

At a junction of three paths, Miss Moser turned to speak to Anne. "I am going to sit in the shade of that bay tree to paint." She pointed to a green ball of a tree straight ahead at the end of the center walkway. "You may join me or take a walk around the garden." Anne felt a little shy to be turned loose, but the thought of meandering through such beauty lured her past her trepidation. She thought briefly of the incident at Vauxhall, but this garden was open and one could see into the next areas clearly. No dark corners and no Lord William.

"It is breathtaking, the flowers-," she sighed. "I would love to walk a little, to see more. Then I will join you."

Anne chose the left trail. Her nose told her there was a garden of mints ahead. She recognized one or two, but the division of the varieties was distinct with sections of white, light pink, purple, and blue flowers at the tall tips. Anne counted eight different mints just in this one section. The smell was invigorating, and the hum of bees filled the space around her with their buzzing vibrations. The sound penetrated her ears until she felt that she, too, might be humming. She felt one with her sweet smelling surroundings.

MISS *Moser's Student*

A hedge of hyssop marked the end of the path where it merged with the other two. Small orange butterflies covered the blue flowers of the bushes. The pungent smell was not altogether pleasing to Anne, but she knew the plant as a friend, having used it for her father's congestion. She had harvested quite a bit of the herb at Lord Greville's manor and left bundles of it tied in the cottage when she moved out, hoping it would keep pests away.

Anne noticed the movement of light colored fabric showing through the branches. There was a woman on the other side of the hedge, stooping to harvest a low growing plant. Anne stood on her toes to get a better look at the worker. The woman wore thin gloves that protected her hands, while allowing her dexterity to use a knife. She was intent on her work and did not notice Anne immediately. Anne kept her gaze on the harvester, so lovely with chestnut hair cascading from under a large brimmed straw bonnet. She wore a light blue muslin dress and a white apron. Anne wished she had such a pair of gloves. In fact, she wished she were this woman, harvesting herbs, and looking so beautiful. She had a vision of her mother, and a warm wind enveloped her.

Just then, the woman stood and smiled. Anne's heart leaped with surprise when she realized it was the same pretty lady she had admired at Vauxhall, John Parker's friend. Now she understood their connection. She decided then that this must be John Parker's fiancée. If his wife-to-be was eager to harvest the ingredients he needed to make his treatments, they were a perfect match. Anne smiled back, embarrassed to have stared so long at the woman.

With the bushes in between and the bees and butterflies flitting about, she could not speak across the hedge, even though she wished to comment on the scene and know the woman better. Instead, she put her hand up in an informal wave and hurried away toward Miss Moser not wanting to disturb the woman's task. Secretly Anne felt a pang of jealousy, and that feeling made her rush away. The turmoil she felt had much less to do with the woman than with a certain man.

Taking the third path leading back to the elderly artist through different herbs, Anne veered to the right at a "Y" in the trail. The perennial plants turned from low clumps to shrubs in this new area. Anne recognized sage as one, but many of the bushes were unknown to her. The air was full of smells that tingled inside her nose as she took a deep breath. She closed her eyes to imagine distant places. As she stood at the junction of the paths in her blind enjoyment, she was suddenly jostled. Branches scratched her arm painfully. She struggled to keep her balance and prevent a fall.

She opened her eyes, surprised and unsettled, throwing her arms out to steady herself with an exclamation, "Oh!" As she was standing there at the junction of the paths with her eyes closed, a man with a huge bundle of herbs on his shoulder had entered the intersection simultaneously. The worker was unable to see her on that side because of his load, and she had not seen the man coming. They collided, though it might have been much worse. When Anne understood what had happened, she knew she was at fault as much as the man who carried the herbs.

The man startled as he felt that he had bumped into something. He suspected a bush, but as he swung his bundle to look, he saw it was a woman. As he turned the rest of the way around, he met the young woman in complete surprise. He dropped his bundle immediately, and came to her with great concern

"I am so sorry, Miss. I did not see you. Have I scratched your arm? Let me see."

There stood John Parker, only a foot away, his sleeves rolled up showing a strong, muscular arm, tanned by the sun. His face indicated he recognized her. She felt she was blushing.

"It is only a scratch. I am sure. I should not have been standing in the path," Anne was quick to say.

"How did you miss my approach, Miss Blake?" He asked.

Anne noticed he knew her name and wondered how he came to know it. She was no longer just "Miss Moser's student". She was embarrassed to answer him, but replied, "I had my eyes closed, taking in the scent of this area. I am sorry, I blocked the trail." Anne smiled, hoping to excuse herself and move off. Then she recalled his gift of the rose water and thought it would be appropriate to say thank you, now that they had met here by chance. She had pondered what to do about responding and this would give her an easy opportunity to do so. "I received your note and the rose water. It was kind of you."

John Parker had sent her the perfume as an afterthought when his father had reminded him of how he had reacted to Anne's last visit to the shop. He had been rude, in fact. He added the gift because he had caught the scent when she had exited. Now facing the woman, he did not want to be reminded of the feisty interchange between them or his actions.

Something about her put him on guard, and he found he wanted her approval. She undermined his esteem. He felt he had to prove himself to her, and he had never let a woman unnerve him as Miss Blake did. He thought to take her arm for a closer look, but could not bring himself to touch her. His heart jumped at the thought of feeling the softness of the skin of her underarm. He scolded himself and looked at her arm without touching her.

"I am concerned your skin has been opened to infection," he said.

Anne pulled the back of her arm around for them both to have a better view. "It is nothing. I will be sure to wash it when I am back at Miss Moser's," she said.

"I am pleased to know it," he said, looking up into her face. He felt her eyes could melt his resolve to stay aloof. It was odd how her manners had softened each time since their first meetings. He could not forget seeing her with Lord Greville though, and the subject tightened his jaw.

"Are you here to collect herbs?" He asked politely.

"Oh no, we are here to paint. I should get back to Miss Moser," Anne said, quickly. He was quite handsome and dressed as he was with his tousled hair, he did not look so prominent as he liked to appear at his father's shop. His gift of perfume and the note had gone a great way toward redemption. She saw him with new eyes. But he was promised to another, and Anne had her heart set on making something of herself and no man, let alone this man, would assist in that, she was sure.

"It is a lovely day for it." He bowed and retrieved his bundle, thinking how he had doubted her story of being an art student the first time he saw her based solely on the condition of her clothing. He had such a different view of her, now. They each walked away in separate directions though their thoughts were on each other.

Miss Moser was a pleasant picture as Anne made her way back to the tree where the artist sat listening with her eyes closed. Perhaps she took in the smells, Anne smiled to herself. She did not wish to disturb the elderly woman. She eased up to her art stand quietly, but the mistress opened her eyes immediately.

"Ah, there you are. You must have enjoyed your walk. I sent Timothy to find you, but you have returned from the other direction. He will return directly and see you have returned, as well." Both women recalled the episode at Vauxhall, but neither would speak of it.

"I met John Parker on the path. It was silly of me. I was standing in the way with my eyes closed as he came around the corner, blinded by a bundle of herbs."

"You were not injured, I hope," Miss Moser said. Anne seemed flushed and breathless.

"A scratch is all, but we were both startled."

"I imagine," the lady said. Maybe this was the new blush she had seen on her protégée's cheeks. "Why were your eyes closed?" The mistress asked, remembering that part of her story.

"The smells were so pungent. I was imagining tropical islands,"Anne said with a grimace.

"I think your imagination serves you well. It helps you with your painting. Now imagine something to sketch, for that is why we are here." The statement was not put to Anne as a reprimand, but as encouraging her back to their purpose and away from the event on the path which the lady recognized as more than just a casual happenstance. The sadness she saw in Anne's face so often had changed to a youthful joy.

Anne took up her paper and a pencil and paused for only a moment before the vision of the lovely woman with the straw hat and thin gloves came to mind. She began to sketch. Once again a strong smell took over her senses and she looked up. Across the trail, an unusual tree seemed to be the source of the scent. The tree was not very tall. The leaves were a bluish green, very pretty. The stringy bark separated from the tree in spots leaving a two-toned coloring to the tree's trunk. The smell was as strong as any of the herb beds. "What is this tree?" She asked, pointing.

"It is called eucalyptus. It came from New South Wales. Sir Joseph Banks donated it to the gardens along with several other shrubs and perennials from his journeys there. It is a scent I particularly enjoy. It has a similar use as rosemary."

Anne's heart stung from the mention of Joseph Banks. Lord Greville's collection of plants that she had spent so much time representing had come from the same man. Why did her past have to interrupt her present so rudely? How would she escape from these constant reminders?

The smell of the tree brought her back to the present. She believed just based on the strength of the aroma it could be very useful for any complaints of the lungs or even a sore throat. The beauty of the delicate tree was equally engaging. She would sketch it as a background to the portrait of John Parker's girlfriend. Anne would enjoy painting the woman even if she envied her in more ways than she would let on to anyone.

John Parker returned for another bundle of herbs by way of the "lovely woman with the straw hat and thin gloves". She spoke before he could, "I believe I saw Miss Blake a moment ago."

"Yes, we met at the junction of the paths. I ran into her, literally. I did not see her standing there."

"Oh dear, she was not injured?" The woman asked with alarm.

"No, merely some scratches on her arm. I don't believe the willow will cause any soreness," he assured her.

"How was it you did not see her or she see you?"

"She had her eyes closed, taking in the smells, she said."

"How delightful! She is an interesting woman. She is here to paint?"

John Parker was surprised that she should take such an interest in Miss Blake, whom his thoughts had focused on for the last few minutes. "Yes", was all he replied, and hurried off to pick up another bundle of branches before his face revealed any of his inner feelings.

The woman noticed his disquiet and smiled to herself. John Parker was avoiding the obvious. Miss Moser's student held more than a passing interest to him.

17

When Anne came down for breakfast, Miss Moser was at the table with her newspaper, her cup of tea, and Edward in her lap.

"Good Morning, Anne. Did you sleep well?" She asked.

"Yes, very well." Anne had grown accustomed to her new life of sleeping until daylight came into her room. Some nights were fitful with concerns for her future, her past, and her latest project, but last night she had slept straight through without a dream she could remember. She took her seat at the opposite end of the table and placed her napkin in her lap.

"There is to be a ball at the museum's hall in two nights time which I will attend, and I desire for you to accompany me.

Anne's chest tightened with fear. She fought to breathe. A ball brought forth terrible memories. She pictured the beautiful white satin dress Miss Moser had purchased for such an occasion. She had hoped she would never wear it, but it appeared that was not to be the case. This was the event the group had spoken of at the tea party.

"It is a charity ball. Everyone attending has paid a pretty penny to be there. The funds will go to the widows and orphans of the Napoleonic campaigns." The matron adjusted her position indicating to the maid to pour her another cup of tea. With that, Edward jumped down. Anne saw he headed to the kitchen, most likely to check his special bowl for scraps.

"If that is your wish-"Anne answered with reluctance.

"Oh, Anne, any other young woman would be jumping at the chance to show off a new gown. It is not a Society event. You do not need to dance if that is your wish, though it may be unavoidable." Miss Moser chuckled to herself, knowing full well that when Anne appeared in the white dress with the lavender robe, she would stun the crowd with her beauty. How different her young student's desires were from most girls.

Anne also had a cup of tea and a poached egg in a lovely hand-painted porcelain egg cup. It had become an every morning custom. Anne was delighted with the overlaid glazes on the cup as she was with the way the egg nested in the hour glass shape of the holder. As she broke the top off the egg, revealing the soupy yolk inside, Miss Moser continued the conversation.

"Juliette and Henry will attend with their aunt."

That fact cheered Anne. Juliette was as fond of this sort of event as she. They were to visit Westminster mid-day. Perhaps they could plan their escape together. Her smile quelled Miss Moser's disquiet, and the conversation left off there.

By late morning, the fog had dissipated, providing a dull sun to the young people's picnic on the cathedral's grounds. They walked through the justice hall which was not in session, allowing visitors. Then they took a more leisurely stroll through the interior of the abbey, humbled by the sanctuary's solemn purpose and the tombs of kings and queens.

"So, much history," Anne remarked to her friends. Even in a whisper, the sound bounced around the walls of the immense interior joining those of other visitors.

"To think, even your William the Conqueror was coroneted in the old chapel," Henry replied. They stood craning their necks back taking in the view, bathed in the colored light of the stained glass windows.

When they emerged into the bright sun, they looked about for a place in the shade. The cathedral's spires cast a vast shadow across the lawn. Mrs. West departed for home, leaving the young people to their picnic. The trio chose a spot on the grass at the edge of the abbey's silhouette.

Though they had planned to sketch the buildings in the future, both the young artists agreed they could not do such a structure justice without serious scrutiny.

"I could never paint such a building," Anne remarked as they sat together eating a variety of small snacks, drinking lemonade, and staring at the magnificent structure. Others across the green were doing the same, while couples and groups of three or four walked the lane to and from the abbey.

"Nor I. All those spires and the details of the windows and carved doors! I have no eye for such a project. I have no talent for perspective on such a view. My drawings always run off the page." Juliette said.

Anne doubted Juliette's statement. She could draw a human face with such believable emotion, a much more difficult assignment. And yet, it chipped away at some of Anne's self-doubt. She felt some pride when she thought of the street scene she had completed successfully. Miss Moser's lessons had been so valuable, but all in all she had accomplished them with little trouble.

"Anne," Juliette began, "there will be a competition at school when I return to Philadelphia. They are accepting all entrants and from those they will choose selections for the show. I would be pleased to take one of your paintings home with me to submit. It would be such fun if we both were in a show together."

Anne could barely resist the beaming smile that she saw on her friend's face. To think a painting of hers in an American art show. But then, Anne's humble better judgment took over. "I could never enter such a competition. I do not fool myself. I am happy making simple pictures for myself and my friends."

"I was thinking of the portrait of Miss Moser's cat. Everyone will wonder what magic spell you used to have the cat sit still for so long." The group laughed.

"The cat, Edward, certainly does sit well. He expects me to do his portrait correctly," Anne said with a smile and again the group laughed.

"No, truly, Anne, the picture is wonderful, the subject is unique and the composition with the flowers, it really is lovely." Juliette assured her friend.

The threesome sat quietly for a few minutes looking out over the lawn. The glow from the low angle of the sun told them it was time to go, yet none of the three hurried to take their leave. They had enjoyed each other's company. Anne worried about the couple's departure back to America. It was a lengthy journey to such a far off land. She wondered if she would ever see them again.

"We will see each other tomorrow night," Juliette said, interrupting Anne's thoughts as if Juliette, also worried about their time together.

"Yes, I will attend, though I dread it," Anne answered.

"You two!" Henry remarked. "The prettiest girls in the country and they fear a ball." He laughed aloud, making his sister blush and put her hand up against his remark.

"We must make a plan to hide together. Whoever arrives first must find the quietest corner and signal the other to join." Juliette plotted.

"We can watch from there and avoid any attempt to have us dance." Anne conspired with her.

"Best of luck with your plan, ladies," Henry stated, shaking his head. He felt sure it would come to nothing of the sort. His sister was indeed a pretty girl in comparison to most, but Miss Blake, Anne, was a beauty that would not be able to hide in any corner of any dance.

When the afternoon of the ball arrived, it was spent in preparation of the evening out. Miss Moser and Anne ate an early supper and started dressing before the sun descended over the horizon. First Millie worked on Anne's hair while Anne waited in her chemise. The goose bumps on her arm were not from chilly air, but from her nerves. Every bit of her body felt tense.

Once again Millie performed her magic, incorporating all of Anne's unruly curls into a twist that started at her neck and ended at the top of her head. Then she wove a small lavender ribbon in and out of the twist accenting the flow of hair. When Anne's hair was completed, she helped Anne into her dress.

Without explanation, a pair of amethyst earrings and a matching pendant arrived on Anne's dressing table. Anne took a peek in the mirror. Standing in her pure white satin dress as Millie clasp on the earrings and fastened the necklace, Anne hardly recognized the woman who looked back. She was certainly not the thin, fatigued girl who had shown up on Miss Moser's doorstep only six months prior.

The woman staring back had a full face from regular meals and no hard work. Her expression had matured as well. Her cheek bones defined the edge of her face, and her eyes were dark even if her expression was bright. Her lips were not thin and chapped, but round and soft. Anne could not get over the changes. They continued underneath her skin as well. She had new confidence even if she felt panic-stricken at the thought of a ball.

As they entered the grand ballroom, Anne tried to control the shaking of her knee caps. She was light-headed and the room began to swirl. She focused all her thoughts on following Miss Moser. She painfully recollected her previous ball; the ball at which she made such an error in judgment.

Lord Greville had come to her rescue, but he had tripped and injured his nose and lip. She had gone outside the hall and the limits of propriety. She remembered his anger and his leaving the very next day for Wales. Had she crushed his hopes as much as he had crushed hers? She would not think of it now.

Her heartbeat resonated in her ears. She took in a deep breath and let it out slowly between her lips. Her toes tingled, not from her new shoes, but from the blood just returning. There would be no fainting.

She would not overstep the bounds of what was proper this night. In fact, her pact with Juliette to sit at the side of the room where they could happily enjoy the evening as wallflowers comforted her. They laughed about avoiding embarrassing moments of being asked to dance by any disagreeable partners, but this is not how the evening would come to pass.

No sooner had Miss Moser led Anne into the room, than a group of would-be dancing partners gathered around. The most aggressive of the group, a tall, thin young man, pressed forward. With coal-black hair slicked straight back from his sharp edged features, he looked menacing. Above his lip was the dark shadow of a new moustache. Anne took a quick look at him and did not wish to look any closer. He frightened her. She could hear him ask Miss

MISS *Moser's Student*

Moser about a dance with Anne, assuming she was her grandmother. Miss Moser held Anne's arm as if protecting her while she spoke to the man.

The line of eligible bachelors was insistent. She could not prevent what she had felt was inevitable no matter how Anne had hoped to avoid attention. Slowly, Anne understood she was about to dance the majority of the evening. Miss Moser smiled at her as the dark-haired young man led her off to the dance floor.

Anne looked over the crowd, her heart racing as she wondered who else might be in the same position as she; a household servant in the past. As she did, there was one person she wished would attend this event, and see her dressed as she was. John Parker was not of this circle of society. As an apothecary, he was a merchant, a business man, and not associated with the upper crust that came to this event, some with false charity, just wishing to be seen. Anne wondered what sum of money was spent to host such an affair, dressed in all their finery, that might have gone directly to the widows and children they purported to be aiding.

Scanning the room, Anne saw that Juliette was having the same difficulty as she. A group of handsome partners gathered around her, as well. Her family was well known and well connected, and Anne knew she would have a difficult time escaping from dancing. They had made a plan they would not be able to enact.

As the orchestra began to play, the circles closed into four dancers. Anne recognized the music and the steps that went with it. She made her body sway past the other couples and rejoin her partner at the end of the line. They danced a pattern to the top again and each time they circled, they return to the original four dancers who moved with them through the dance. As the tune finished, they all congratulated each other, and the dark haired young man led Anne back to where Miss Moser and her next partner waited.

18

By the time the first set of dances were completed, Anne had experienced the skills of several different young men. She was so thirsty that she could not smile and she found it hard to speak. Her last partner was a short, stout man with a sweaty brow and an odd odor. They joined the crowd at the one side of the room in order to find the refreshments. As neither Anne nor her partner knew what was available, she followed him with her arm resting on his. As Anne spied the plates of small cakes, cookies, and bowls of punch and lemonade, her mouth watered. At the far end were decanters of cider and wine drinks for the older couples.

"What would you care for, Miss Blake?" he asked.

"A glass of lemonade and a small piece of cake would be nice," Anne answered. She moved away from the crush to allow others to push into her vacated spot. She stayed to the side and felt someone very close behind her, uncomfortably close. As if pushed from behind, the person's arm slipped under hers in a familiar way. She immediately tensed at the reminiscent gesture. The crowd would protect her, she reasoned as she turned around. When she saw whose arm had taken hers, she was astonished by a face so out of context she almost failed to know it.

"It is you, Anne! When you were dancing, I asked myself, who is that pretty girl? I kept trying to get a clear view of your face, but then I saw you walking this way and I knew. What a surprise!"

"Lord Andrew, how good to see you." Anne gave the young man a broad smile, truly happy to meet him. Andrew was Lord William's younger brother. As a child, he had been one of Anne's pets, a good little boy and not at all the trouble maker his older brother had been.

"I am so glad to see you are doing well. In fact, I am most astounded to see you here. Your father-."

"My father passed last winter and by a kind gesture I have been sent to live with an aging artist here in London."

"I am so sorry. Wait until I tell Willie you are here!"

Fear squeezed the breath from Anne's chest as the thought of seeing the lord's brother overtook her. She leaned back against the wall to steady herself. She felt as if she might bolt back to Miss Moser and then run all the way back to the safety of her room.

"No!" Shocking Andrew with the vehemence of her exclamation. "No, you must not. We have met twice already. I have no reason to see him again."

Lord Andrew was well aware of his brother's gallivanting ways. He could imagine the rude behavior that might have put Anne off. Although William had not mentioned seeing Anne recently, in the past, his brother had always spoken of her in demeaning terms. Odd as it was, his brother seemed to speak of her more than any of the other maids.

"As you wish." Lord Andrew assured her. He saw the worried look on Anne's brow and how she looked over his shoulder with concern, so he added, "I doubt he will come in here. I left him playing cards and drinking too much in the outer room. He leaves for his Grand Tour in the morning, so he has only this one last chance to make a fool of himself in town."

Anne's stout partner returned. He bowed to Lord Andrew and Andrew bowed in return. It seemed they knew each other. "Enjoy the dance," Lord Andrew said moving off as Anne tried to calm her shaking hand enough to take a sip of lemonade.

Returning to Miss Moser, Anne saw that her next partner, a large man with a great quantity of brown hair, was waiting and speaking to the lady with his back to her. She took a deep breath trying to control the emotions that shook her so violently moments before. When her next partner turned, Anne was relieved to see it was Henry Harris. She had not seen him in the crowd.

"Awe, Miss Blake, how lovely you look," he said with a wink. "Are you enjoying the dance so far?" He teased her with his formal tone, knowing full well how she might answer if she could.

"Not as I should, I suppose," was all Anne could say, worried that tears might follow as she was so relieved to be in Henry's care.

Her friend led her to the dance floor, and they began to follow the patterns. Anne was disturbed by her meeting with Lord Andrew, but kept a small smile on her lips as she proceeded through the dance. As they circled each other and returned to their original spots in the line of dancers, Anne caught a view of the opening into the card room at the far side of the ballroom just in time to see Lord William make his entry. She craned her neck to keep an eye on him as she made another circle around Henry and back. She wished the dance would end and she could retreat. Lord William was approaching along the wall straight toward her. She could not tell if he had seen her, but her anxiety increased with each step the lord made in her direction.

At last, the music ended. Anne thanked Henry for the dance and took his arm, pulling him off the dance floor awkwardly. There was no time to explain her haste to leave the area, hoping the lord would not spot her. Before they could return to Miss Moser, however, Lord William met them and pushed his way in between Henry and Anne, separating her to stand alone.

"Ah, Greville's whore!" he said loudly enough for many to hear, as he took her arm. "May I have the next dance?" He stumbled into Anne, pulling her back toward the dance floor. It was obvious that he was drunk.

Henry came quickly in front of him cutting him off from further advancing to the dancing area. He looked at Anne and saw the expression of horror on her face.

"I do not believe that the Miss wishes to dance with you," Henry said politely.

"What do you know of her?" Lord William asked. He sneered at Anne.

"She is a friend of mine. You have insulted her and us who know her. Please step away."

"If you wish to make friends with a gardener's daughter, a whore, and mistress to Lord Greville, that is your business. I have business with her as well. She has caused me shame and trouble. She owes me an apology and a dance."

Henry assigned no merit to the man's remarks, and continued to block the nobleman's way.

"As I said, Sir, she does not wish to dance with you. Unhand her, now," Henry stated firmly, not backing down.

When Lord William did not do so, but laughed instead, Henry delivered a punch that not only removed the man's hand from Anne's arm, but sent him sprawling onto the floor. Women screamed, and several men moved forward to help the lord up and away.

The scuffle ended and the music started up slowly so that the dancing could resume. Henry took Anne to the side of the room where Juliette, their aunt, and Miss Moser made a protective barrier around her. A group gathered to console her. Some knew Miss Moser and some knew the wickedness of Lord William. Anne did not cry, but uncontrollable spasms came from deep in her chest, making it difficult to breathe. After a minute in her protective circle, she calmed down.

Miss Moser took Anne gently by the shoulders and looked at her squarely, speaking in a quiet voice as the others moved off to dance. "I know you are upset, but it would be best if you made your way back onto the dance floor with your next partner. Show everyone that you have no cause to be alarmed by anything that has been said. Give it no value by returning to enjoying the evening." Miss Moser turned to find Anne's next partner waiting patiently behind her.

"Ah, here is your dance partner. Please_," she said indicating for him to join Anne and return to dancing. Though reluctant and still trembling, Anne moved forward to the dance floor with her next partner, a gentleman a bit older than most of the crowd of men who had asked to have a dance. She had a quick thought of Lord Greville. As the music began, Anne ordered her feet to follow the steps while displaying the most difficult smile she had ever produced.

When the dance ended, it was Henry Harris who waited for the next dance. Anne was so glad to have a chance to speak to him. The dance was not as boisterous and fast paced as the previous ones. Partners faced each other for most of it, so Anne had a chance to remark on his well placed punch.

"Thank you so much for coming to my rescue," she said, as she met him with a hop.

"That is my specialty, don't you know? I rescue damsels in distress!" Henry smiled a full smile, happy to have used his boxing skills for such a noble purpose. He admired Miss Blake. He had sensed she might have come up from a less fortunate beginning. As an American, however, Henry knew class distinctions were becoming blurred. One could move up in society much more easily than here in England where there were books keeping track of it all. It was extraordinary that she might have been a gardener's daughter, but it seemed likely due to her keen interest in plants. Certainly, he held no disregard because of her upbringing. He had no interest in her as a suitor, either. He felt so much more than that. A life-long friend was worth twenty romantic interludes, in his estimation, and he felt Anne might be such a friend.

As Anne made her way around the dance floor, secure in Henry's arms, she felt safe. It was a feeling that she realized she longed for. She would hope that when she found a husband, he would make her feel this way. She wondered what John Parker might have done in this situation. If someone insulted his beautiful fiancée, would he have stood up for her so valiantly?

As Henry returned Anne to Miss Moser he asked, "Better, now?"

"Yes, thank you," she replied with a smile all for him. She did appreciate his care.

Henry barely could release her. Not only did he enjoy the jealous looks from the other men watching them dance, he also wished he could escort Miss Blake for the rest of the evening, assuring that no one else would harm her or even come close.

19

*I*n the morning, there were seven calling cards on the silver tray in Miss Moser's front hall. Two of the cards had nosegays of forget-me-nots attached. In addition, there were three invitations to soirees over the next week. Anne came down to breakfast reluctantly. She was wishing she could stay under her blankets and linger there all day. Hodges passed her the tray, and she looked through the pile with horror. The invitations addressed to Miss Moser and Miss Blake were especially frightening.

Miss Moser did not come down for breakfast, but took the meal in her room. Anne sought her out as soon as she finished the little food she could bring herself to eat. Her glum face must have shocked the elderly woman. "My dear, whatever is the matter?" Anne passed the matron the tray full of cards, etcetera, and said, "I am not prepared to receive callers or attend these parties, however

147

well meaning or perhaps curious these people are." With that, the tears came.

"Sit down here, ah, the outburst of the young lord last night still has you upset. No one believed any of the young man's remarks to be true," Miss Moser said.

"What he said was true! I am a gardener's daughter. No, I was not Lord Greville's mistress, but I would have been had he asked me."

There it was Miss Moser remarked to herself. She had believed all along that a relationship beyond Anne's drawing for the nobleman had been the reason she was sent from Lord Greville's household.

"You might have been exposed to ridicule and shame had the truth come out," Anne replied.

"Only from the shallowest of acquaintances, I assure you, and I am beginning to doubt whether it would matter. Society is changing, and the strict roles therein are loosening their tight reins on opinions. You are no longer a gardener's daughter. We will not look at your upbringing as limiting, but a special beginning to honing your talent. You are no longer just a gardener's daughter, but an excellent artist."

The elderly woman's comments still did not reassure Anne that the door to society would open as the cards on the tray seemed to suggest.

"Anne, if you do not believe you are different, then you will never be so. It is your own perception that is important. How you see yourself will reflect how others see you."

Anne did feel different. Dressing for the ball, she had seen a notable change when she looked in the mirror. All her life, she had felt different, but the acts of Lord William and her misunderstanding of Lord Greville's intentions had made her less sure of that feeling. She would never be sure there would not be another person ready to expose her. She had come from common stock, and that could not be changed.

"We can avoid these invitations easily enough if you prefer. Hodges will tell any callers that you are fatigued and staying abed. With time though, you will need to come out of your shell and see that these are opportunities for you." Miss Moser held the tray of cards up to Anne.

Anne took the tray from her and thumbed through them again as Miss Moser poured her a cup of tea. She paused at one. The note was from Henry. He did not have a traditional card, but used one he obtained from his aunt. On the back he had written Anne a note. "My dear Miss Blake, It was indeed my pleasure to come to your assistance last evening. Please know you may call me to rescue you anytime- Your humble servant and friend, Henry." Anne separated the card from the rest as it held a special place in her heart. She would keep it always as a reminder of the evening and what had occurred.

"Do you know whose card is whose?" Miss Moser asked.

"I suppose I do for a few." Anne picked out four of the cards. "I believe Lord Cheswick was the short man who sought refreshments for me. I remember dancing with Mr. Phillips. The dark haired man was Mr. Carroll, and of course Henry's note, I recognize. The others, I am not so sure," she answered.

"Let me see," Miss Moser reached to take the remaining cards from the tray and identify each one, telling Anne what she could about each. The invitations were from three of Miss Moser's friends, wishing to include Anne in their circles.

"Although you might wish to avoid exposure, by not attending you may just be qualifying the young man's comments. I will give you the afternoon to collect yourself, but it would be wise to respond to these invitations, at least."

After her tea, Anne rose to return to the solace of her room. She gave Miss Moser a peck on the cheek before going upstairs. "I do appreciate all you have done for me," she said quickly, trying to hold back more tears. Miss Moser took her hand replying, "I have done little other than offer opportunity. You have done the rest by being such a good student and a graceful and lovely young woman."

In her room, Anne stared out the window at Miss Moser's small garden behind the house. Her blurred vision recalled Lord Greville's rose garden and Anne let tears fall down her cheeks as an old ache returned. She remembered her resolve and blotted the tears away as she went to work in the studio.

She had finished her painting of Edward. In fact, Miss Moser had taken it to the shop to have it framed. Anne had accompanied her to the store to help pick out the mounting and the wood for the frame. There had been several different woods, but in the end, they selected a light oak that matched the beige of the cat's fur.

Miss Moser showed Anne the various papers appropriate for watercolor from which she asked her to choose a few. The matron gave the man behind the counter the dimensions for three new canvases to be stretched. In addition, she collected a small pile of brushes; insisting Anne should have her own.

With the new supplies, Anne decided she would use watercolors for her painting of the woman collecting herbs. Anne felt a jealous excitement picturing the woman. The creation of her painting satisfied that emotion. It took her mind off her distress. She thought perhaps she could give the painting to the couple as a wedding gift when the time came. She resisted recalling the image of John Parker's arm, muscular and tan. She shivered remembering how he almost touched her arm. Would she have swooned had they touched? Possibly, she smiled to herself.

The actual drawing of the woman, an outline of her straw hat, her hands with thin leather gloves, the flowers and the pale leaves of the eucalyptus tree took only an hour to complete. She had not tried to draw the woman straight on, worried that unlike Juliette she would not be able to capture the sweet beauty of the subject of her envy. The composition pleased Anne.

Once or twice she heard Hodges making her excuses at the front door. She felt a pang of guilt, but stayed from the window, lest she be spotted from the street below. Late in the afternoon, Miss Moser came to the studio. She saw her student hard at work on a new painting; satisfied her art would help heal her sore heart. She bent to look at the new work on which Anne concentrated so diligently. Miss Moser was impressed with how the subject took up the foreground at a pleasing angle.

"What a lovely image. Where did you get the idea?"

"She was harvesting herbs at the Chelsea Physic," Anne replied. "I believe it is John Parker's fiancée."

"His fiancée? I did not know he had plans to marry. He speaks mostly of a trip to America soon. I wonder if she is to accompany him." Miss Moser thought to herself without saying aloud that the woman in Anne's picture looked a great deal like John's sister, Alice.

"Miss Moser," Anne called to the mistress as she opened the door to leave, "are you aware that Millie has a talent for sketching?" The mousey housemaid was elsewhere, so Anne had braved the subject in her absence.

"No I have not heard of it, but of course she is a good maid, and so quiet."

"It is true. I have given her my old paints. I believe she pays close attention during my lessons and has the ability to replicate what she sees in a wonderful fashion. I was hoping she might show you her work. She is very shy about doing so, remarking she would not want to bother you."

"Oh nonsense. I will certainly request a look at her drawings."

"Thank you," Anne said. She was thinking of her own good fortune and how Miss Moser might be able to help Millie, if not to the extent her luck had run, at least for the girl's own enjoyment.

20

*M*iss Moser returned from her meeting at the Royal Academy. She found Anne in the studio still working on her painting of the woman and the herbs.

"Good afternoon," Anne said as the mistress came into the room. "Your meeting went well, I trust?" She asked nonchalantly, knowing that Miss Moser had dreaded the meeting as there was a chance her opinion of who should win this year's awards might meet some argument.

"Yes, quite well. They agreed with my recommendations." She mentioned that the committee had spent a great deal of time deciding this year's awards. Even so, the members were apt to have different opinions. "I am going to have tea, remove my shoes, and sit quietly for a bit. Come join me if you are at a stopping point."

She seemed out of sorts to Anne. She was tired, most likely. Anne stopped her work and cleaned her brushes.

When tea was served and Anne sat attentively at her side, Miss Moser began a conversation she was eager to have with the young woman. "I spoke with several of the group who were concerned that Lord Greville has taken ill. He has not attended any meetings, and word has it he does not fair well." She looked up to catch Anne's expression, and indeed it was full of concern. "I thought perhaps you would like to know."

"Did they say what ails his lordship?" Anne asked.

"Yes, someone, I don't remember who at this point, did say it was his stomach that pained him."

"I am aware he has had a problem in the past. It must be somewhat serious for him to miss meetings," Anne remarked.

"Yes, that is why I mention it. Perhaps you wish to send a note to him, a get well wish."

Anne knew she would like to, and by Miss Moser's suggestion, the lady would facilitate it with postage or a messenger. Anne thought to do more than a note, though, and dared to ask for her mentor's help.

"I would like to send him some herbs from the apothecary. Perhaps he has a tonic."

"That would be thoughtful. It may be that the Parkers have already made a preparation for him. You may have an idea of an herb for his stomach? You may use my account, if you would like."

Anne could hardly wait until the morning arrived to set out to the Parker's establishment. She was intent on choosing a cure for Lord Greville, but she also had a secret desire to see the young apothecary again. She might impress him on her knowledge of stomach medicines. As she came through the door and the bell tinkled to announce her arrival, the scent of the small store came over her once again. This time she was prepared. She took a deep breath of the place, delighted to return.

It was the older apothecary who came out to greet her. Anne saw John Parker's fiancée working in the back room. She certainly appeared to be entrenched in his life and business. Anne could not form an ill opinion of the woman when she sent such a lovely smile her way from beyond the curtain. The congeniality of her expression came with a familiarity as if the woman was already acquainted with her.

Though Anne had seen her at the pleasure garden and more recently at Chelsea, collecting herbs, they had never spoken. And yet it was odd to think the model for her painting had no idea she was being portrayed. Anne thought she might say something, but then reconsidered. The woman was just the basis for the painting, not a true portrait. She would not admit to jealousy as part of her decision.

"How can I be of assistance, Miss?" James Parker recognized the girl as not only the one who accompanied Miss Moser, but also as the one who had annoyed his son. To have caused such a reaction from John was unusual, but now looking into the lovely face and intense eyes, he could imagine why.

"Yes, Sir. I am interested in a tin of candied ginger. Do you carry such a product?"

"Yes, yes, here it is," he said, reaching under the glass counter. "Many use this for freshening breath."

"I was thinking of it as a way to soothe a sore stomach," Anne said.

"Many use it in such a way. Anything else?" He asked.

"Yes, I would like some balm, a small bit for tea," she answered.

The man was so agreeable. Anne found his demeanor and helpfulness so different from the younger man. His eyes twinkled as he spoke to her, and his kindness put her at ease. They continued to discuss some other possible herbs for the tea Anne sought, comparing their knowledge and stories of success using certain combinations.

"You are Miss Moser's student, is that correct?"

"Yes. She said you would put my purchase on her account," Anne answered timidly.

"Of course. Will you be taking the package with you?" He asked.

"No, I would like it sent to the Right Honorable Charles Greville at Paddington, if you would."

"Yes, certainly. I was not called to attend him as he has a different physician, but I am happy to be assistance from afar. We are well acquainted. We both enjoy looking at rocks," the man said with a sense of humor. "He has quite a collection."

"I lived at his manor for a short time. My father was the head gardener. Lord Greville was kind enough to show me several specimens in his collection." Anne spoke without thinking. Both her admission to being the daughter of a gardener and to being so familiar with Lord Greville might reflect negatively on both she and the lord.

The apothecary did not seem to react to the information. "How kind of you to think of him. Your father grew herbs?" The apothecary wanted to learn more about this gardener's daughter turned art student.

"It was my mother who had the knowledge of plants for cures," Anne said. She felt humbled by the man's sincere inquiry.

"Ah, and have you drawn the herbs as well?" He asked.

Anne realized he must know something of who she was as the questions were so correct. "Yes, for part of my stay at his lordship's I did some paintings of the flowers in his hothouse and some of the plants in his garden, though I did not spend so much time drawing herbs.

"My son plans to travel to American to collect herbs and study the native culture. He has no talent for drawing, but he will bring back what he can and perhaps make sketches of the rest."

The man finished wrapping and tying up the package for sending out. "I will see that this is delivered as soon as possible."

"Thank you," Anne replied and gave him a smile of gratitude that was meant on many levels. "What are the dried berries in the bowl here?" Anne pointed to the shriveled red berries that sat to the side under the counter with a price indicating they were something special. She did not recognize them to be any fruit she had ever seen.

John Parker had returned to the shop through the back door. When he realized it was Anne to whom his father spoke, he stayed to the side of the curtain to listen to their conversation. When he heard Miss Blake's request for the package to be sent to Lord Greville, he turned away, sickened at the thought of the young girl with the elderly lord. He did not listen to what else she said until he heard his father mention his journey to America and the young woman ask about the berries. He entered the front room quickly to respond.

Anne looked up at his sudden entrance. She was not in the mood to tangle with the young man today. He came to the counter and pulled the bowl out to let her have a better look.

"They are cranberries, collected from bogs in America and then dried. They are excellent for the kidneys." John Parker wanted to impress the woman. Yet, once again he felt he fell short of his mark.

"Oh, that would explain the price; so dear." Anne said, keeping the conversation light.

"I plan to sail to America to see such plants for myself," John Parker proclaimed.

"With a wife?" Anne was surprised at her lack of guile, but the young man answered without a pause.

"No, I will travel alone," he said without wondering about the question.

Strange, Anne thought. She wondered if the lady with the lovely smile in the back room was aware of his plan. Some part of her was pleased to hear his fiancée would not accompany him. Another part was disappointed at the man's planned departure. Though she enjoyed her situation with Miss Moser, she was well aware that an end was inevitable. Another change would come for which there could be no prediction, no plan.

This man could make plans. His life could go on. For Anne, she could not make a plan or predict her part in the future. He would go to America, and she would-.

"Thank you for your help," she said to the older man, and smiled at the younger. John smiled back with the same twinkle that Anne had seen in the elder apothecary's eyes. It was a pleasant change, and Anne knew it went far in increasing her admiration of the handsome doctor. They would not battle today. John Parker ran to open the door for her, "Good day," she heard him say above the tinkle of the bell.

When John turned back, his father was puffing on his pipe, filling the area behind the counter with a thin layer of blue smoke and the sweet smell of burning herbs. The woman also poked her face through the curtain from the back room.

"She came for something for Lord Greville?" John asked his father to clarify.

"Yes. Kind of her." The father remarked.

"I suppose that is what mistresses do," the younger man said.

"I don't know about mistress, but she did say her father had been Lord Greville's gardener."

"No!" The son exclaimed, looking toward the door as if he would still see her. "That is amazing."

"Well, for you to think she is "amazing", now we really are getting somewhere. Your mother will certainly be planning the wedding," he chuckled, turning to the young woman who continued to smile at the two men from around the curtain.

"Pshaw." The young apothecary spit, embarrassed to be teased about a subject closer to his heart than he cared to admit. He thought back over the short conversation he had just had with the woman. How strange that she should ask if he would travel with a wife. Not a usual question. He wondered from where her inquiry came.

He was proud to speak of his upcoming journey. He felt brave speaking of it, but in fact some part of the ocean crossing was quite frightening to him. He did not dwell on it, but rather liked to think of wandering in the woods, viewing plants unfamiliar to him and perhaps meeting a savage. He had most of his steerage money already. He was saving all he could from his earnings for his services. He did not wish to land in America without a sum of money on which to live. He felt by the next spring, he would have money enough for the journey.

Anne met Millie outside the shop and hurried down the street at a quickened pace. It was all Millie could do to keep up. Anne's thoughts tossed between concern for Lord Greville and the apothecary's remarks about his trip to the New World.

When Anne arrived home, Miss Moser was sitting in the drawing room. She had a society paper and a magnifier in her hand. She looked up to see Anne coming in.

"You were able to purchase what you wanted, dear?" She asked.

"Yes, the apothecary was very helpful."

Miss Moser wondered if she referred to James or John, but did not ask. She noticed Anne's face as she sat in the chair opposite hers, looking out the window. "Do you think a visit to Lord Greville might cheer him up?" She asked the pensive girl.

As if knowing her thoughts, Miss Moser had addressed Anne's inner desire to see the lord; a thought she had as they made their way back from the shop. She was not sure there was anything she could do for him, but she longed to know the extent of his condition.

"Would that be possible?" Anne asked. Her voice almost cracked thinking about Lord Greville.

"Certainly," the matron replied, happy to give the girl some relief.

21

*A*s Anne descended from the carriage that Miss Moser had hired, she remembered her arrival to Lord Greville's estate a year ago. Today, she asked the driver to leave her at the beginning of the lane that led to the house. She wanted to walk from Paddington Green to Lord Greville's manor to revisit what she had seen so many times before. Though she had lived here less than a year, the surroundings; the giant elm trees, the oak lined drive, the birds in the hedges, were all so welcoming as if she were coming home. The time she spent here had been of greater significance than her entire previous seventeen years when she lived on the Duke's estate.

Coming back to this manor where she had worked on drawings for Lord Greville, lived with her dying father, and had her first taste of higher society made her realize how much she had changed and how she would never again be that person. She felt older, wiser, but with a loss of innocence. Yet, in many ways she was in the same position as she had been then. She waited for Miss Moser to open the doors of society for her so she might go in. What would happen if those doors shut? Could she return to work as a nursery maid? That is what frightened her most. When Miss Moser was finished with her teachings or in the event something happened to the elderly artist, what would become of her? Where would she go? These were all the same questions she had asked herself when she lived here. She had been saved that time. She left off her thoughts as she climbed the step to the large wooden door, the servant's entrance, on the side of the manor.

Anne entered the house as quietly as she could. She saw Cook before the ruddy faced woman saw her. This ambush had been the other reason she wanted to be left off far from the house; to surprise the kitchen maid. Anne tiptoed up to grab the large woman in a hug which the Cook initially resisted, but eventually returned.

"Oh, Anne!" She said, trying to catch her breath. "I knew you were coming, but I thought you might come to the front door." She stepped back to look at Anne's attire.

Anne was wearing her newest walking dress. It was a stunning combination of dark and light blues. Velvet accents of the darker color wrapped around the wrists, formed the collar, and circled below her bust. She wore her straw bonnet with a dark blue ribbon to match into which she had stuck several sprigs of lavender. Cook made a sweeping motion with her hand down her young friend's clothing, indicating how amazed she was. She smiled at Anne's good fortune.

"You look so lovely. It is good of you to visit the master," Cook said.

Anne looked down her dress. "It is new. Miss Moser has been so good to me, and I owe him so much for what he has done for me," Anne replied, referring to Lord Greville.

"He received your package and has spoken to the hall maid several times about it. He tells her stories of your time here. She listens though she does not know you."

Lord Greville heard Anne's voice in the hallway. He shouted out, but Anne and Cook could not tell what he said.

"Will Mrs. Lambert announce me?" Anne asked as that is how she had always visited the master in his library previously. She would be announced by Mrs. Lambert when Anne was called before the master because of some trouble she had caused.

"Oh dear," Cook cried out. You have not heard. Poor Mrs. Lambert has gone to meet her maker. She died last month."

It had been over a month since Anne had seen Lord Greville at Vauxhall, though he had not mentioned any illness at that point. Anne felt estranged from this household. It was sad to hear of Mrs. Lambert's passing, and sadder still that she had no knowledge of it. That is how things were with servants. No one ever talked about them. You didn't hear ladies say "oh my upstairs maid has taken ill and died". No, usually the passing was only noted as inconvenient as a new maid was sought and trained.

"Is Sylvie about?" Anne asked after the housemaid with whom she had been the closest.

"No, Sylvie went to work at the same estate as her sister. I believe she missed you greatly." Anne hated to think she might never see Sylvie again in her life, but of course she had felt that way about the entire household when she left to live with Miss Moser.

"I should go to him," she said to Cook as they heard Lord Greville call out again.

"Yes, he will be so pleased to see you."

Anne met the new downstairs maid in the hall heading for her master who had called out. When the maid saw the lovely lady, she stepped aside to allow her to enter.

"You must be Miss Anne," she said.

"Yes," Anne answered, pleased to have the girl familiar with her.

"He tells me stories about you. He speaks as if he hopes I might draw flowers for him one day, but I can't make a circle, I tell him. I am so glad you have come."

"I am glad you listen to his stories. He was very kind to me."

"He is a good man, but so weak now with his illness. I heard the physician tell his brother that it would not be long now."

Anne tried to keep her emotions in check. She assumed his situation might be dire, but she had not expected to have that fact clarified by the maid.

"I am happy to hear of his time at court and all the famous people he knew. He says you liked to ask him about it, too," the maid continued.

"Yes, I was fascinated with his stories and he taught me all about rocks, flowers, and the stars." Anne thought of the night she had been sitting out on the lawn and the lord had come out also. It had been an accidental meeting and the beginning of a keener connection between them.

The two heard the master make a noise again. They had been almost whispering in the hall. It was time for Anne to go in. The maid held the door for her and she put on her best smile as she entered.

Lord Greville straightened in his chair from the slump into which gravity had pulled him. He looked out the window, guessing the time to be late morning. He had spent most of the last few hours dozing. He had already taken a tincture for pain two times. He worried his grimaces would put Anne off when the pain returned, but he did not dare take another dropper of tincture for fear he would doze off while she was present. He did not wish to miss a moment that he could spend with the young woman.

M I S S *Moser's Student*

When Anne came into the room, he was struck by memories of previous visits she had made to his library. He had been quite the master then. Now, he was just a crumpled old man. Oh how he ached for his younger body.

Anne was shocked at the nobleman's appearance. He had lost a great deal of weight. The old sadness she had seen so often in his eyes had a deeper set to it. He looked completely worn out. He battled his pain, she supposed. She felt such pity, but produced a smile instead.

"Ah, Anne, you look so pretty," Lord Greville said with all his heart. He was amazed at the transformation from young innocent girl to a beautiful young woman with a proud demeanor, something she had always possessed. The distance between their ages had grown from a small stream to a wide river. He had made the right decision; sending her away to Miss Moser. If she had stayed, she would be taking care of him now.

"Lord Greville, it is so good to see you, though I fear you have not been feeling well of late." Anne stated the obvious, but she could not help but say what her heart was feeling. She was so saddened to see him so wasted. She could tell that he was barely able to lean forward in his seat as he indicated the chair next to his for her to sit.

"This stomach of mine has been having its fits. Really nothing but cramping, yet it barely subsides between episodes. I don't wish to dwell on it now, though. Come sit and tell me of your lessons and how your life with Miss Moser is progressing. She is a fine teacher?"

"Yes, she is much more than a fine teacher. She has been wonderful to me. I have been lucky with teachers my whole life," Anne began as she took her seat, careful to arrange the skirt of her new dress. "When I lived with the Duke's family, the children's tutor was very kind and gave me lessons beyond the work of the younger students. Then, I was fortunate to have a teacher who taught me much about flowers, the heavens, and rocks." Anne laid her hand on Lord Greville's arm as a thank you, for it was he of whom she spoke. "Now, I have Miss Moser, who not only instructs me in painting, but also about life. She is very wise and has guided me well."

"A teacher appreciates a good student," Lord Greville remarked. "How is your life, Anne? We barely spoke at the Gardens."

Anne wished she could lie and say, "All is well." But she could not. The episode at the gardens and now at the ball and her involvement with Lord William had reminded her of her place in society. It was more than that, though. Her relations with John Parker had been awkward, also. She wished it had been more pleasant, but he was engaged to another and even a friendship had not developed. Juliette and Henry were lovely people and perhaps her only friends, but they were bound to other places in their lives; events that would eventually leave her behind. She knew that. She was really quite alone even if she had people around her.

It was more than loneliness that was bothering her, and she wondered if Lord Greville truly would understand. She was a gardener's daughter. They could not change that no matter how they dressed her or where she was seen.

"I have enjoyed my time of course, but I am still alone in my life. You paid me more mind than anyone since my mother. Miss Moser does so as well, but she is not my age, or similar to me in very many ways. I have made few friends because I am meant for a different destiny, I believe."

Lord Greville did not follow Anne's meaning. He watched her speak, admiring her beauty and thinking of how close he had once been to her, kissing her, in fact. He sensed her sadness and knew that she would open up to him if he asked. He might be able to advise her if she needed. It had not been so long ago they had spoken in this way.

"I am not sure to what you refer. Your destiny, your happiness?" He waited for her to explain.

Anne pulled her thoughts together. She would tell the lord the truth. He deserved nothing less for what he had done for her. Her anger at his turning her out had long since vanished. Now that she saw how ill he was, she worried that she should have been responsible for his care. She wondered if she could have done anything that might have saved him from his illness. She wondered if she had stayed-.

"I was born to service. I am meant to work and maybe even work hard. It is not in my nature to be idle or lazy. I have no desire to be so." As usual her words sounded as if she had thought them through before speaking, but she had not. Her thoughts were an epiphany as she explained her complaint to the nobleman. He drew the realization from her.

"I have learned so much of the process of art and how to recreate what I see. Miss Moser says that is our gift."

"Yes, you have an eye for detail and the pictures you made of my flowers were indeed very fine. Their quality did not fall short of any I have seen elsewhere. I am sorry I never had the chance to tell you so until now. Had they not been destroyed by the maid's jealous act, I would have shown them proudly to my fellows." The lord looked away as a cramp squeezed his intestines cruelly.

Anne saw the edge of his face and knew his pain embarrassed him. She hurried to keep speaking to allow him to pause.

"When I made the drawings for you, it was so fulfilling. I had purpose. There was a reason for my artwork, not just passing the time. That is what I need. I wish to make a difference, not just pretty pictures."

"Then find the reason. Do the work. As a woman it may be more difficult, but like me, there are others who have need of your skills. Remember we spoke once of the old herbals and how childlike the drawings are. Perhaps you can work with an apothecary or such to make a new herbal."

It was prophetic. Lord Greville knew nothing of her relationship with the Parkers, but there it was. James Parker had mentioned his son needed an artist. He was going to collect plants in America and not taking his lovely fiancée. If she could show her skills, maybe she could contribute to his success by recording them not in America, she had no money for such a journey, but when he returned.

"Thank you, my lord. As usual our conversation means so much to me. I will find someone of the sort. Thank you for being my mentor, for sending me to such a wonderful teacher, and for always giving me confidence." She leaned her head on his shoulder in a way she would have done with her father. That is how she thought of the lord, now.

"I should have done more," Lord Greville sighed softly, patting Anne's head as they stayed just so for a minute. When Anne sat back up, she asked about the garden, gave her condolences about Mrs. Lambert, and told the master about the ball. She did not tell him about Lord William or the cards on the silver plate in the morning, but kept the conversation light. She spoke of Henry and Juliette and how nice it was to have friends her own age. They talked about America and the idea of so much unexplored ground. Lord Greville spoke of his wish to go there that would never be fulfilled. Lord Greville called for tea which Cook brought in.

"Doesn't our Anne look quite like a lady, master?" She asked.

"Yes, indeed," he answered, looking over at the young woman who sat so close, yet who seemed so far removed from him now.

They were quiet with their own thoughts as they drank the tea. Anne wishing she could do more and Lord Greville wishing he could stand and walk Anne through the garden.

Anne hated to leave, but she knew he would summon for more pain relief as soon as she took her leave. As they said their goodbyes and Anne leaned down to embrace the lord, she saw the look in his eye that told her once more that he had loved her. She kissed his cheek slowly and then stood. She had loved him, also.

"You must not let me down on using your art for a noble purpose. I expect nothing less from you," he teased. His last look at her made him draw a breath of pride.

"I will let you know what I have found. Be well," Anne said, knowing he would not.

On her way back through the kitchen, Anne was happy to see Cook's husband, Lucas. They had a short exchange of news, and then he left his wife to say her good-bye. As Anne hugged Cook one last time, they both shed tears. Anne stepped carefully down the steps out the back door as her vision was blurred. She walked down the lane to the square where she would meet the carriage home. She knew this was the last time she would come to this manor on Paddington Green and the last time she would see Lord Greville.

22

*I*t was only ten days later that Miss Moser came home from a meeting at the Academy feeling dread at giving Anne the news. It seemed sudden, even if they all believed it was inevitable. Millie was sent to find Anne who was reading in the library. Lately, her curiosity about America had her reading anything she could find on the subject. Although the library was small, she found an article by Thomas Jefferson, and another about the natives living along the eastern coast. Each account referred to the vast tract of land to the west, yet to be explored.

Now she found a newsletter from a missionary, telling of vast lakes and a river much wider than anything seen before. Anne was aware of Lewis and Clark's Voyage of Discovery. There was little of what they found published as of yet, Lord Greville had shared some hint of the oddities they had encountered in the natural world of their exploration.

"Mistress has returned and wishes to speak to you in her parlor," Millie said when Anne looked up as the maid finally located her. Anne put the pamphlet down and followed the maid up the stairs.

"Ah, Anne, how have you spent the afternoon?" Miss Moser inquired, allowing Anne to settle into a chair next to her.

"I have been reading in your library. I found a few articles concerning life in America. I wish to learn more about the new country. Everyone speaks of the wild landscapes there. It intrigues me."

"Yes, there are opportunities for many there," the lady responded.

Anne thought of John Parker's intentions, but she said nothing of her thoughts. She waited for Miss Moser to begin a conversation as she had summoned her for a particular reason.

"Anne, I have some very sad news. Lord Greville has died."

A force knocked the air from Anne's lungs. She gasped to pull air back in, her stomach too tight to help.

"It occurred two days ago. I was informed at my meeting today. Everyone was shocked, though I know you were aware of his stomach problems. His condition was much more grave than many suspected."

The recent visit, how sickly Lord Greville had appeared, and what the new maid had overheard the physician say came rushing back at Anne. Perhaps she, better than some, had realized how sick he was. She supposed he kept the extent of his illness from most of his acquaintances. Without being rude, Anne wished to be alone. The pressure in her chest was becoming unbearable. Sobs would follow. "Excuse me," she said, stumbling from the room.

Miss Moser watched Anne's exit, knowing the pain the young woman suffered. The two, the nobleman and this amazing gardener's daughter, had been very close. She did not know all the circumstances and possibly would never know them, but she knew love when she watched it. The emotion in Lord Greville's eyes at Vauxhall that day, and look in Anne's eyes just now told her the extent of the love they had felt for each other. Miss Moser knew Anne's pain; she had felt such agony when her husband died.

Anne stretched across her bed, letting the tears flow at will. She cried for her lost life. She cried for her father's master. She cried for the man who had taken such pains to include her in his world. She cried until exhaustion overtook her and she drifted off to sleep.

The dream started with the lulling, swaying of the waves. She could see the deck of the huge ship shifting from one side to the other. The rail on the right approached the water and then lifted to the sky as the rail on the other side ducked toward the water. Then it was up to the sky with a new wave. There was only one other person on the deck of the ship with her, and she knew it was Lord Greville. She made her way to where he stood to remark on the view, a far off land mass. The sea birds screeched above them, and a salty water spray misted her face.

Anne wished to share the experience with Lord Greville, knowing he would have knowledgeable contributions to her otherwise innocent enjoyment of the voyage. As she eased along the side of the ship, hanging onto the railing as tightly as possible, she came to stand near the nobleman. When she looked up to speak to him, she was surprised to see it was not Lord Greville at all. Instead, she was standing very close to John Parker. He looked over at her, equally surprised. He called her name. As she was about to answer him, she started to come awake.

Anne woke with a jolt, realizing Millie was knocking at her door and calling her through a small opening. "It is time for dinner, Miss. Will you come down to eat?"

"Yes, Millie, thank you." Anne answered.

She felt such warmth from remembering her nearness to John Parker. The dream seemed so real. It was almost dark outside. She had not lit a candle before falling asleep. An aching cramp tightened in her stomach as she remembered that Lord Greville was gone from this world forever. It felt so strange to think of life from now on, knowing he was no longer at Paddington. She had counted on that fact. Once again, the cord that ran from her past to her present was severed and it frightened her.

She recalled her dream and wondered at its content. On the end of her bed, Edward sat with his one leg pointed up in the air, while he cleaned his stomach. His licking rocked the bed, and Anne realized he was the lulling movement she had felt on the ship.

"Thank you, Edward. It was a wonderful dream." She had not thought about her reaction to seeing John Parker on the deck of that ship, but now wide awake she knew it had been pure delight.

Miss Moser considered what she might say to comfort the girl, but nothing of substance came to mind. She knew each person grieved in their own way. She would wait to see how deeply Anne's sorrow dwelled. She was relieved to see a small smile on the girl's face as she entered the room.

"How are you feeling, Dear. I am so sorry for your loss."

"He was in such pain when I visited. He is at peace now. It is selfish to be sad." She chastised herself. "He was so kind to me. Thank you so much for letting me visit him. I think we said our good-byes that day."

Miss Moser did not reply. What Anne had said was so wise. We who are left behind are sad for ourselves. Those who believe in Heaven cannot feel sad for the departed. She had tried to remind herself of the same when her Hugh died. What was different for this young woman was that she had lost so much. Her father and mother were gone. She had no siblings or other relations. Anne had been sent to live with her under unusual circumstances, and no one knew what the future might bring. Undoubtedly, it would worry Anne. When Hugh died, she still had her uncle, her nephew, and many friends on whom she could depend. This girl only had her.

"There will be no service. I imagine he will be laid to rest in Warwick, unless other arrangements have been made. With no wife or children, his estate may go to his brother, Robert, I suppose. I am so glad you were able to speak to him when you did. You two were so close." Miss Moser would leave it at that. She did not wish to distress Anne further.

Anne sipped at her soup, forcing herself to eat. She thought of her cottage at the back of the nobleman's property where she had left her mother's chair. She wondered what would happen to the lord's house, his garden, his hothouse of plants, and most of all the bureau of rocks in the library she had once spent a day polishing.

23

The mysterious parcel arrived by courier. Mysterious because the man insisted he was to give it directly to Miss Anne Blake. Hodges directed the man to wait in the hallway, while he summoned Millie to locate Anne.

Millie went straight upstairs. Anne was in the studio sketching a tall ship from a print she had found in Miss Moser's library. This drawing in particular had spurred her curiosity and even created the backdrop for her dream. After all, she had never seen a tall ship or the ocean, for that matter. Drawing the waves and the clouds on the far horizon intrigued her, but the boat's details were difficult, and she hated to give it up. She could place the ship further back, but what would be the subject of the drawing? A whale? Millie's arrival was a pleasant interruption.

"A package has arrived for you, Miss." Millie said. " Hodges has asked for you to come downstairs to the front hall."

As Anne descended the stairs she saw the man in uniform with the rather small parcel in his hand. Hodges came forward and said, "Sorry to disturb you, Miss Anne, but this man has instructions that you, and only you, are to receive this package." Hodges or Millie might have been curious about the contents of the package, but it was not their place to inquire.

After the man handed over the box and departed, Anne debated opening it right then and there. She saw that the package came from Paddington, so she went back upstairs to her room. She considered a private viewing might be more appropriate. She could only imagine what was in the box.

When she was removing the string which had been tied securely to hold on the lid, Anne felt her hands shaking. She lifted the top to reveal a thick layer of tissue pressed tightly into the box. She caught the edge of the thin paper with her finger nail, lifting it gingerly, only to find several tissue wrapped items inside. She recognized the wrapping as the way Lord Greville had kept several of his mineral specimens.

Unwrapping the first of the small gifts, Anne was astonished to find a small red stone, a ruby. It was the very stone Lord Greville had shown her the day she knocked a mineral cluster from the greenhouse window sill. He had been so kind in showing her about crystals rather than reprimanding her for the mess she had made. She had worried that she had broken a diamond. Now she knew better. She could look at a crystal and understand just a little of its formation. Lord Greville had given her that.

She put the ruby on her desk to unwrap the next ball of tissue. This time the stone was blue, a sapphire. The blue was interrupted by a silver star that moved about on the polished surface. Anne remembered to breathe, putting the blue stone next to the ruby. The third stone was a piece of the tourmaline from Derbyshire, a local specimen she had admired. She was proud she also recognized that the fourth gift was a chunk of calcite crystal. Lord Greville had explained that it always broke into cubes. The last package was tucked into a small velvet pocket. Tied to the pocket was Lord Greville's card. Along the bottom was written, *"The diamond I never was able to give you is yours at last."* CFG

When Anne turned the card over there was an entire message on the back.

Dear Anne, If you are receiving this note, then I was not able to deliver the box myself. As you can see, I have included the minerals from our day in the library. These stones are not to hold onto as some sentimental gesture. They are to be sold, and the money used to help establish you in a better situation. You could travel or attend art school. The money could support you while you paint. These stones can be your dowry. Please do this for me as repayment for all that you and your father did for me. Your humble servant always, Charles

Anne dabbed the tear that splashed on the edge of the card. The pressure inside her throat strangled her. She let out a primal howl of pain and sorrow. He had thought of her as he was dying. He had provided for her in the end. Why had she ever been angry with him when he was thinking of her best interests all along? She was ashamed.

She opened the velvet bag and let a very large diamond roll out onto her palm. It was almost blue, the stone reflected light so well. Anne knew nothing of diamonds except that Lord Greville had told her they were the hardest of all minerals. The light captured inside the stone was mesmerizing. He had told a little of the faceting. She took the gem to the window for more light. It sparkled in her fingers. Though she had seen only a few diamonds in her life, this one's brilliance and size let her know what a prize she held. Carefully, she returned the stone to its velvet home.

Anne smiled a bright smile for herself. The sobs were gone, instantly traded for an epiphany she came to in that moment. She knew exactly what she would do with the gems. She was only sorry it was so late in the day; too late to act on her decision.

Millie knocked on her door and announced tea time. The afternoon had raced by while her life took another sudden change. It was difficult to believe what had just occurred. She carefully replaced the stones into their tissue nests and back into the box they went. She secured the lid on the treasure box. Anne took a quick look in the mirror, straightening her hair, and dabbing the damp tear tracks from her cheeks. She looked at the woman in the reflection and barely knew her. This was a new Anne, a woman of means looking back. She examined her face seriously, wondering if she deserved such good fortune. She took up the box and went to Miss Moser's room.

"Come in dear. I have heard you received a package. Of course I am curious, but it is your business entirely."

Anne stepped forward and handed Miss Moser the box. "Please," she said indicating for the matron to look inside. Miss Moser took the lid off the box. She removed the tissue and began to unwrap the small gifts one by one with notes of surprise and an "oh my" as she did.

"They are a last gesture from Lord Greville." Anne felt a bubble of sadness building in her throat again, but she smiled through it.

"These are beautiful gem stones of the highest quality I would guess." Miss Moser rolled the ruby and then sapphire around in her hand. When she picked up the calcite she said "I do not know this mineral."

"Lord Greville gave me a mineral lesson one day in his library," Anne began to explain. "I mistakenly thought this common mineral, calcite, was a diamond. These are the very same stones we examined that day and two more. It is so unexpected. Read the card, if you wish." Anne remained silent while Miss Moser read the note and then opened the velvet pouch. "Such a sparkle," she said. "He has given you quite a gift. These will bring a good price and give you money enough to give you choices about your future." The matron thought back on her concern for Anne on the day Lord Greville died.

"I am thinking of helping someone else," Anne said staring out into space. She was thinking of a tall ship and on the rails at the side she could see a man with ruddy cheeks and chestnut hair; proud, intent, and happy to be sailing to America.

Miss Moser saw the look in her eyes and had an idea to whom she referred. She wondered what the young woman had in mind, but she would not inquire. She would be in Anne's confidence when her young friend thought it best. Perhaps she was still considering her decision, whatever it was.

In the next moment, however, Anne spoke up. "I will offer to sponsor John Parker's journey to America. I know he will be discovering new plants and new medicines for the good of all. The sooner he has the money needed for his trip, the sooner those recipes will be available to those who need them."

It all sounded so altruistic, but Anne had additional considerations she wished to include in the sponsorship. She would discuss her idea with the young apothecary as soon as she could visit him. The look on his face and the knowledge she had helped him were two of the pleasures Anne looked forward to from sharing her gift. She hoped his fiancée would not feel the gift inappropriate. Rather, she hoped they could be good friends, establishing a relationship with the apothecary into the future. How her emotions would deal with such a connection is something she did not wish to think about.

"That is very kind of you, Anne, but you may want to think a bit more about your future than how you can help John Parker. He will have his fare soon enough, and may refuse your offer out of pride." Miss Moser did not want to disparage her student, but she did want Anne to be prepared for a quite different reaction from the one the young woman was imagining.

Anne definitely had not thought through her idea to the end. The notion that he might refuse her gift had not come under her consideration as of yet. It had been such an unexpected gift, she could not think only of herself. She thought how much she would love to share it. When she thought of sharing it with someone, there was only one person who came to mind.

24

*T*he next morning, Anne could not resist the desire to see John Parker a minute longer. She wanted more than anything to tell him how wrong she had been. They had started their relationship with misunderstanding and mistrust. It was time to end all that and start anew with the friendship she felt for the man.

She asked Miss Moser if it would be acceptable for her to venture out to the apothecary's shop after lunch, and if Millie would be available to accompany her. Miss Moser whole-heartedly agreed, believing this to be the breakthrough for which she had been hoping. Miss Moser knew Anne was wary of a connection to the young man based on all that had gone on before. She was anxious for the girl to have this opportunity to offer assistance to John Parker. Miss Moser was so pleased that Lord Greville had chosen to make sure there was a secure future for Anne.

The two young women headed to the shop early in the afternoon. Anne did not dawdle at any of the shop windows. Her eagerness to see the apothecary pulled her forward in an incautious manner. The girls wove their way through the streets, so busy with delivery wagons parked on each side. Men were loading and unloading goods, forcing the women into the street. The two dodged one wagon as it came down the street at a fast pace. They hung back waiting to cross until that wagon had safely passed. When Anne looked down the street with a clear view of the apothecary shop, she stepped out into the road without any thought of what might be coming from the other direction.

Anne heard Millie scream, and then all went dark. As the cart came swiftly around the corner where Anne crossed, the driver tried to swerve to miss her. His load shifted and two large crates fell from the side. As the boxes slid off, they tumbled along the ground before they came to a stop. The first one knocked Anne down, and the second rolled over her, hitting the side of her head. The man stopped his horse as soon as he could and jumped down to find the crumpled form of a lady in the middle of the street with his boxes and their contents strewn about her.

There was much shouting and other women screamed as Millie ran to the apothecary's shop for help. When she arrived breathless, John met her on the front step of the shop having heard the commotion outside. He caught her as she almost fell across the threshold. He did not wait for her to catch her breath to explain. He recognized the maid as Miss Moser's, and the horrified look was all the explanation he needed. The woman hurt in the street was Anne.

John Parker ran up to the crowd that formed a tight circle around the injured woman.

He knelt down beside her unconscious form.

"Please step back," he said. "I am a physician. I will tend her."

There was blood along the side of Anne's face, but it did not appear to be coming from her ear. He was thankful for that. Her breathing was short, but steady. He ruled out a broken neck or severe head injury. Though Anne was unconscious, the blow had not been fatal. As gently as possible, he tucked his arms under her limp body and rose to carry her back to his shop. There were murmurs in the crowd about the woman's condition and what had happened. Everyone agreed the driver had taken the corner at too great a speed, but also that the woman had not looked before she entered the lane.

John Parker carried Anne through the front of the shop to his living quarters beyond. He knocked a pile of books off the sofa and slowly bent to put Anne down. Millie followed close on his heels opening and closing the door to the shop and helping adjust a pillow under Anne's head before the apothecary released her. He kept the wound side up so that he could staunch the bleeding and care for the cut the edge of the box had caused. He worked quickly grinding a poultice and gathering bandages. He passed Millie a basin and pointed to a pitcher on the nightstand. As she dabbed at the source of the blood the young doctor saw that the cut was superficial, but the blow to the side of her face where the corner of the box had clipped her was turning a light blue indicating a substantial bruise in the making.

He stopped the bleeding by applying the slightest pressure for a minute and then applied the poultice and a fresh bandage. His hands were shaking as he gently moved her head onto the pillow. He was never nervous, he told himself, but he also never treated someone for whom he cared so much. He directed the maid to fetch more fresh water with which he began to wipe Anne's brow in an attempt to cool the beginning of a fever. He instructed the maid to continue as he heated water for an infusion.

He sprinkled chamomile and feverfew blossoms, mint leaves, and a bit of myrrh into the mortar and ground the mixture into a fine powder with nervous agitation. He dumped the mix into the hot water and allowed it to steep. He placed comfrey leaves, lavender flowers, and yarrow into a bowl with a little vinegar, stirring the combination into a new bowl of water for the maid to sponge on Anne's brow. The drying vinegar and the aromatic herbs would help cool her head and reduce swelling around the hot purple lump that continued to rise from Anne's temple. Though she did not wake during these treatments, her breath remained shallow, but steady.

John stood and looked his patient over as he thought of what he could or should do next. He felt so helpless. When the back door to the shop opened, he was relieved by the woman's arrival. It was the same woman Anne had seen at Vauxhall, Kew Gardens, and here in the shop. Anne had assumed she was the apothecary's fiancée.

"Miss Blake has had an accident. She received a blow to the head from two crates that fell off a wagon. It seems to be only a bruise, but we must watch the swelling and hope to wake her soon." He walked in circles, agitated and unsure.

"I am here, I will stay with her as is proper. Send the maid to notify Miss Moser. We will await her instructions. She will know if anyone else should be notified about Miss Blake's accident. Then we can make a decision about a surgeon," she instructed.

As Millie ran out the door, John saw the driver of the cart standing outside holding his cap in his hand and bowing his head as if praying. He could tell by the man's posture that he felt great remorse for what had happened. John went out to speak to the man.

"I do not feel the injury is grave, but she has not come awake as of yet. She has suffered a substantial blow. We will know more in the next few hours. You are welcome to inquire in the morning." He returned to Anne's side and spoke softly while the woman was busy straining the infusion.

"Please wake up, Anne. My heart cannot stand to think I will never tell you of my feelings, my sweet girl," he said in a raspy whistle, full of emotion. He took her hand into his. "Our stubbornness has robbed us of time we should have been together. I could not see my true feelings for you because you challenged me. How right you were that even the most common things can be wonderful. You spoke of the groundsel, wild on the edges everywhere, yet an important herb." He bowed his head, thinking of their confrontations and how sorry he was for them now.

"The girl who came into my shop appeared to me to be a common housemaid. I met the lovely art student with doubt and mistrust. Yet you demanded my respect with your knowledge. Oh, I have been so blinded by prejudice. I have wasted so much time I could have spent with you. Now, I worry you will never wake." He bent to kiss her hand imagining her lips instead.

The woman re-entered the room, but seeing the intimate position and the murmur of his voice, she held back, allowing him this time alone.

As he sat up, he saw Anne's eyelids flicker. She moved her head and moaned lightly. His glad heart's excitement rushed through his entire body. She would live, and he would love her. He waved forward the woman in the doorway. She looked up at the ceiling and said a quiet, "Thank you."

The couple watched together as Anne opened her eyes to the bright room that circled around her and made her squint. Oh, how her head ached. She saw vague forms. One moved off to close a curtain that dimmed the light allowing her to open her eyes once more. The other form came into focus.

It was John Parker. A sharp pain throbbed in her head when she tried to think. She could not conceive of where she was, and why of all people she should see John Parker. Was she dreaming?

"Miss Blake, Anne, you have had an accident," he began slowly. Anne closed her eyes to listen to what he said. "Boxes fell from a cart and you were struck down, suffering a blow to the head."

Anne felt she should surely sit up to speak to the man. She began to try, but his hand was on her shoulder holding her from rising.

"You must rest. I have sent for Miss Moser." He produced a dropper of tincture from the bottle next to her bed. "Take a bit of this, it will ease the pain. I will not give you very much as I do not want to lose you again."

The apothecary squeezed a few drops onto Anne's open mouth, at the back of her tongue. It burned as it flowed down her throat. The pain in her head began to lessen almost immediately.

Anne heard a conversation and wondered who else was in the room. When she saw the woman standing there with a cup, she closed her eyes again. Seeing the woman caused a pain that had nothing to do with her accident.

"Here, take a little of this tea. I have added a little honey for the bitterness," the pretty woman said. Anne opened her eyes and saw them crouching close together. She let the woman pour a sip of tea from a spoon through her parted lips. She felt the tea chase the tincture down the sides of her throat. She relaxed back onto the pillow, unable to fight or to resist or to think any ill thoughts about the woman who nursed her. The apothecary continued to speak in a soothing voice.

"We are here and will not leave your side. The maid will return with Miss Moser soon, and we will decide what is best at that point."

Anne nodded with her eyes still closed and allowed the opiate he had given her to erase her pain.

After a quarter of an hour, a chaise pulled up outside the shop where there was still a small crowd assembled. Miss Moser hurried in. John met her at the hallway door, leading her back through the shop into his darkened private quarters.

"She is in here," he indicated to the elderly woman.

MISS *Moser's Student*

Miss Moser came to Anne's side and saw the bruise and bandage. She realized the severity of the injury and turned away from the young woman, placing a handkerchief over her face as she starting to sob. Anne had fallen asleep, not back into unconsciousness, but she appeared motionless as if dead.

"Will she recover?" the Mistress asked. There was a crack of concern to her voice.

"I believe so. She awakened and understood a bit of what has happened. Although the blow was serious, the placement was fortunate as the corner of the box fit between her temple and the top of her cheek. She might have broken her jaw had it hit any lower or been killed immediately had it struck her temple. The cut is not deep. I have given her a tincture for pain, but she will hear you if you speak."

Miss Moser sat on the chair John offered and bent close to Anne as she patted the girl's hand. "Anne, you are going to be alright. You must rest and let the Parkers take care of you." Miss Moser could say no more as the sobs returned. She rose to move to the other side of the room to speak to the apothecary out of earshot of his patient.

"It does not appear that she should be moved. Millie will stay to aid you with Anne's care in any way possible. I will send over a few of her things. Tomorrow we can decide if she should be taken elsewhere. You do not believe we should send for a surgeon?"

"I think she will come through this fine, but if I am alerted to any variance from what I believe to be normal for such an injury, I will certainly send for Dr. Thomas. I will continue to administer the tincture for pain, herbal tea as she is able, and apply cool lavender wash to her head. Should we notify her kin?"

"She has no living relations," Miss Moser answered.

"What about her connection to Lord Greville?" John was still unsure of Anne's relationship to the recently deceased nobleman.

"No, there was no arrangement of any sort. Whatever gave you that idea?" she asked, curious that the apothecary would inquire.

"I saw them together at Vauxhall."

Miss Moser smiled at the young man. She remembered that day. She recalled how strange it was the young apothecary never looked her way after Anne returned on Lord Greville's arm. No wonder, he had been jealous. Many things had happened that day, but becoming Lord Greville's mistress had not been one of them, though no doubt some part of the nobleman had wished it so.

"Ah, I see," Miss Moser mused. "No, Anne was not his mistress. She lived at the lord's manor and did some botanical paintings for him. Her father was Lord Greville's head gardener."

John Parker was stunned. He had assumed so much that was wrong.

"I was under the impression Lord Greville sent Anne to live with you in order to polish her manners in the same way he was supposed to have prepared Emma Hamilton."

"He did send Anne to me for art lessons, but there was never a plan for her to return to him. I believe he gave both Miss Blake and Lady Hamilton up for the same reason. He surrendered them in order that they might have a better life. I think he loved Anne enough to sacrifice his own desires for what would be a better situation for the girl." Miss Moser blotted the last of her tears from the corners of her eyes.

"I feel certain she is in good hands, now," she said, placing her hand gently on John Parker's. "How fortunate that she was coming to see you when the accident occurred."

"To see me?" The apothecary asked.

"Yes, I believe she wished to end your squabble. It is about time you two realized that you are in love," the elderly woman said pointedly. She looked at the young man's face which flushed at the mistress' comment.

M I S S *Moser's Student*

"Are we going to be the last to know?" the young man asked the lady, surrendering to the truth.

"Yes, I think so," the woman added from behind him. She was smiling at Miss Moser as she came back into the room.

"Hello, Alice," Miss Moser said to the woman, returning her smile with one of her own.

25

*A*nne stirred as the light of morning came through the windows of the shop. She had rested for sixteen hours and impatiently waited for daybreak the last two. Though her head still ached a little, it was not the pounding pain of the afternoon before. She was glad she was only a little dizzy as she sat up in the bed. She saw Millie curled up like a cat in a chair at the foot of her bed. The maid must have worried so.

As soon as Anne sat up, Alice came to her side. Alice had been so kind and attentive, seeing to her needs throughout the night. Her voice was soothing, her touch so gentle, but Anne had no wish to watch her nurse interact with John Parker. What Anne had witnessed so far indicated they knew each other well and coordinated their efforts in a way Anne could not criticize or ever hope to equal. They made a good pair.

"I would like to return to Miss Moser's as soon as it is possible," Anne said as Alice took a seat next to her.

"Yes, of course, if you are certain, but it is no trouble for you to stay," the pretty woman assured her.

It was obvious to Anne that Alice was reluctant to have her leave. "I appreciate your care, but I can rest there just as well without interrupting your day." The more kindness the woman bestowed upon Anne, the more Anne longed to get away.

"Do you remember that you were coming here yesterday when you were injured?" Alice asked.

"No," Anne answered slowly. She tried to think of how she might possibly have been in the area. Discouraged that nothing came to mind she said, "I don't recall anything. I suppose Miss Moser sent me. I will inquire when I am home."

Alice did not want to pressure Anne, but she knew Miss Moser had not sent Anne because it was the elderly artist who mentioned Anne wanted to end the squabble with John. Alice knew her brother's thoughts on the young woman had changed over time. She hoped the chance for reconciliation had not passed. She wished she could stall Anne as her brother had gone to treat a patient on the other side of town, an emergency in the night, and her father would not be in for another hour.

"How do you feel? Is there any dizziness?" Alice tried to think of the questions her father or brother might ask.

"No," Anne said. "I feel quite well. The pain is only a dull ache, not the sharp pain of last evening."

"Would you care for a little something to eat before you go?" Alice asked. She looked over at Anne's maid who had not eaten since yesterday afternoon, but Anne shook her head.

"No thank you. We can wait to eat until we get back to Miss Moser's. We hate to bother you any further."

Though she tried to stall Anne from leaving, there was no delaying her departure. Finally Alice called for a coach to take Anne and Millie home. As the pair traveled the short distance to Miss Moser's, Millie passed Anne the box she had retrieved from the street.

"I knew this was important to you, and so I made sure to pick it up after the apothecary arrived to attend to you."

Anne remembered the box and then slowly, the contents. Out of the fog of the accident, Anne remembered why she was carrying the package. A flood of emotions and realizations washed over her, and she could not control the wave of tears that followed. She was not sure why, but everything seemed dismal. Her life had once again proved to amount to little.

Anne knew her injury and seeing John Parker and the pretty Alice was affecting her reasoning, but she could not stop a deep longing from surfacing. Sometime, she would have such a relationship. Someday she would have such a man for a husband. She would, she assured herself through a blur of tears.

"Oh, Miss Anne, you have been through so much. Here, we have arrived."

Indeed they were at Miss Moser's door and everyone was on the steps to meet her. Hodges came forward to assist her out of the carriage and into the house.

Miss Moser saw Anne's wet cheeks and thought perhaps the young woman was in pain.

"You may rest down here in the library," she offered.

"No, I would prefer to go to my room. I will be alright. I am just a little tired. I will nap for a bit."

Miss Moser followed Millie and Hodges up the stairs to the girl's room. She wanted to remind her of her resolution yesterday, but then thought better of it. She wondered if something had changed. For now, Anne needed to rest as she indicated. There would be time for questions later.

Anne was thankful for the solitude of her room. She really was tired, but moreover, she needed time alone. She remembered why she was on the apothecary's street. She had intended to approach John Parker about making drawings of the samples he brought back from America. She thought to inquire about the fare for passage to America. She wanted to let him know she had money enough for him to pursue his dream.

Watching John Parker work with his pretty fiancee and how the two seemed to know each other so intimately made her shy to the idea of approaching the apothecary with any of her intentions. Now, her offer seemed out of place and insensitive to his fiancée's feelings. Miss Moser's words came back to her. Anne's thoughts were much clearer now. The injury to her head jostled her vision and her plans.

Tears rolled down her cheeks as she thought of Lord Greville and his gift. She would use the money from the gems to improve her future, but how? Who would hire her to do drawings if her abilities were unknown? She would speak to Miss Moser and seek her advice. For now, she was tired, very tired.

Crawling onto her bed, she waited for sleep to come. After turning her body around three times, struggling to relax her mind as much as her body, she gave up. She was agitated and needed to speak to Miss Moser at once.

"Come in dear," Miss Moser answered the familiar knock on her door. "That was a short rest," she said as Anne came over to her.

"I was not so much tired as needing a few minutes to gather my wits."

"Ah, yes, I understand." Miss Moser hoped this referred to her speaking with the young man.

"May I ask for your opinion?" Anne asked as she sat in what had become "her" chair.

"Certainly, you know you can," Miss Moser replied.

"As you know, the gems will benefit me financially. I am aware that money could open doors that status cannot. I am perplexed as to my future. I have never had the ability to think of independence, and yet here it is placed at my feet."

"So what do you suppose you might do?" Miss Moser was puzzled by the young woman's intensity. Where she should have been overjoyed at the options, she seemed morose. "What is it that troubles you so?"

"I have an idea to provide my abilities for drawing botanical drawings for engravers much as I did for Lord Greville. I wonder who would hire an unknown artist."

Miss Moser wondered if this was truly what was bothering the girl? She seemed so upset.

"There are ways to expose your artwork. There are activities at the Academy, art shows, and even competitions in which you could participate. I have connections and can act as a reference until you are established. I think it an excellent idea that you return to drawing flowers as a source of income, but do not limit yourself to just that. It is your interpretation of what you see that is so wonderful. I think of your painting of Edward, for instance."

"I was thinking of John Parker's journey to America. His father says he will bring back samples. I thought perhaps I could make a record of what he brought back. I thought of working on an herbal at some point. The old herbal's drawings are so hard to use for identification. It is an idea Lord Greville put forth to me when I visited." Anne paused before going on, pulling her thoughts together and remembering her conversation that day.

"I would be happy to be of service in that way. I enjoyed drawing Edward, but I do not think I was given my gifts to draw only for pleasure. I believe I am to draw for such a purpose."

"So, you did not speak to John Parker about your idea?" Miss Moser asked.

"No, it did not seem proper. His fiancée was there at every turn. Such a wonderful person. I realize now that I cannot work for Mr. Parker without acknowledging that I find his annoying ways attractive. I have worked for a man I thought I could love once, and I will not torture myself again."

"The attractive woman," Miss Moser raised her eyebrows, "is she the one in your portrait of the herb gatherer?"

"Yes, I saw her in the gardens that day, so lovely with her auburn hair under her wide-brimmed hat, her gloved hands, and all the flowers. I decided she would make a perfect study."

"That, my dear friend, is John Parker's sister, Alice. He is not engaged to anyone at this time."

Anne could barely take in what her mentor was telling her. Yes, the woman's name was Alice. His sister? His sister! Then, he was not as good as married. As quickly as she could, she thought of all the glimpses she had of the Parkers together. Each and every one did not convince her otherwise. Looking back, it was entirely possible that she had misinterpreted their relationship all along.

Miss Moser watched the smile that spread over Anne's face as she realized her mistake.

"So now will you tell John Parker your idea?" The elderly artist inquired.

"Yes, and I will also let him know I am rich and able to sponsor his journey to America in exchange for the chance to illustrate a book about what he might find!" Anne glanced at the clock, but it was already afternoon; too late to ask to ride to the apothecary shop. She would have to wait until the morning, she thought of her mistake and this time, laughed aloud.

Miss Moser was happy to hear the laugh and the general shift in Anne's mood. Her student had entered her room a sad and melancholy soul and now left with great mirth.

26

It would be difficult to wait until the morning, but Anne would rest easy now. She knew her plan and with the extra knowledge that John Parker did not have an intended after all, she felt there was hope for her future. This time when she stretched out on her bed, she was asleep in minutes. She slept so deeply that she did not hear someone had arrived to Miss Moser's front door. She did not wake when a young physician inquired about his patient upstairs. It was only when she heard Miss Moser knock softly on the door to her room that she came awake.

As Miss Moser entered the room, she noticed Anne looked beautiful. There was solace in place of her usual sadness. "There is someone to see you, your physician, I believe," Miss Moser said with a wink. "Should I show him in?"

"Oh," Anne startled. "Perhaps, I should come down." Anne sat up, patting down her hair. This time she did feel dizzy and the room was spinning. Before she could say anything more, the door was pushed open and John Parker stood at the foot of her bed.

"Or perhaps, not. You rest right there," he scolded with a smile.

With those words, Anne lowered herself back on her pillows and closed her eyes for a moment. She no longer felt her head, but now it was her heart that seemed dizzy. She opened her eyes again to see John Parker had moved closer.

"I do not wish to disturb you, but I must know if you are alright," he implored. "I was absent when you made your departure. I was surprised to find you gone when I returned." John Parker sat in the chair at the side of the bed. He indicated he wished to take her pulse. Anne held her arm out and tried not to shudder when he took her arm and touched her wrist. He took a magnifier from his bag and looked into her eyes asking, "How is your head, do you have much pain?"

"Other than the bruise on the side, no constant ache as I did last night," Anne explained. She tried not to look back at him while he studied her so closely.

"I think you will mend and be much more careful when crossing streets in the future," he said lightly.

"I was coming to see you," Anne said more bravely than she would have believed possible only hours ago.

"Yes, that is what Millie said."

"You are planning a trip to America when you have sufficient funds. I recall our conversation," Anne began.

"Yes, that is my hope," John Parker replied.

"I was coming to tell you that I would like to sponsor you on your journey. It seems I have come into a bit of money."

"A bit you should save for your own purpose," John said humbly.

"Oh I have a price," Anne said. John Parker looked at Anne with amusement. He wondered what she could possibly mean. "I wish to be the one who draws the samples you bring home with you. Perhaps put them together in a book."

"Very interesting idea. The only problem is that I planned to be gone for two or three years. I could send samples home, but I could not guarantee their condition."

Anne thought of all the boxes of plants she watched her father unpack; plants sent on even longer journeys under more difficult circumstances. Moreover, she was dealing with a new disappointment at the duration of his trip to America. He might never come back or marry a woman over there.

"I suppose that would be a possibility. I have seen plants transported in my past. Lord Greville received plants from all over the world that my father carefully unpacked when they arrived."

John Parker held his chin with one hand and his elbow braced his arm with the other while he thought of his answer. He knew what he wanted to say. His next words might be the most important he would ever speak. He must take care to say it correctly. His eye caught Miss Moser slipping out the door. She must have sensed the moment.

"Or, you could come with me to America," he said, looking directly into her face.

Anne was surprised. She realized now that she had always dreamed he would ask her, but never thought it would happen because of his supposed betrothal. She did not think he had money enough for his own passage let alone for another. Now all that had changed. He had no wife-to-be, and she had money to pay not only his way, but her own as well.

"Come with you, as your botanical artist?"

"No, Anne," he said as he bent down on one knee beside the bed. "Come with me as my wife."

Anne had only a moment of consideration before she nodded as tears rolled slowly down her cheeks. The young apothecary leaned across the bed and took his patient into his arms as their lips met for their first kiss.

Millie came into the room unexpectedly. She had brought fresh water for the basin and a stack of towels. She backed out of the room as quickly as she entered it and ran down the hall to Miss Moser's room. The matron caught her as she came through the door.

"Isn't it wonderful?" Miss Moser asked the maid who was all giggles.

"I am so happy for Miss Anne." Millie said, hugging Miss Moser and then doing a quick jig.

"Yes," Miss Moser responded. "She will be the apothecary's wife!"

27

They had a simple ceremony. Miss Moser stood up with Anne, and John's brother stood with him. The elderly artist had arranged for the bishop to marry them. He was older than Miss Moser and had a smile that assured Anne she was marrying with the blessing of God, himself. Miss Moser had explained that the bishop had been noted for his continued sermons about the abolition of slavery. He was a liberal minded clergyman with a reformer's attitude concerning the church. He preached against the use of pleasure gardens and such on Sundays.

Miss Moser had been able to convince him to marry the pair even if they were not members of his parish. The matron explained Anne's arrival to her home and found that the bishop knew Lord Greville from his connections to the royal family. Miss Moser indicated that the funds for the couple's trip had come directly from Lord Greville which the bishop found fortuitous.

Anne was able to contact Cook and Lucas. They had been asked by Lord Greville's brother to stay on at the Paddington estate until matters were settled. When they heard the news of Anne's marriage they accepted the invitation to attend immediately, sending a note back with the messenger.

Anne wrote to them once more to ask Lucas if he would walk her down the aisle. Anne could not think of anyone who could stand in for her father. Although Lucas worried that he might disgrace her somehow, Cook assured her husband that not only was he specifically asked by the bride to be, but also it was Anne who had done the asking, and they were as close as anyone living to the girl.

After the ceremony, Miss Moser gave a party for the couple at her home. Anne presented Cook with the painting of the street scene, and John gave Lucas a penknife. It was a gesture that John had thought of on his own. It endeared her husband to her even more. Juliette and Henry were able to attend. Their journey back to America was scheduled only a few days later. Their Aunt and Uncle West attended also.

Anne was happy to see John Parker engaged in lively conversation with the sister and brother. She heard Henry joke with him about his choice for a wife. Henry and Juliette showed genuine interest in John's intentions once they arrived in America. The foursome promised to reunite on the other side of the ocean in three month's time. Juliette did not take the portrait of Edward, as Anne felt she should leave it with Miss Moser, but instead took Alice's portrait which Juliette promised to return after the show.

Alice, too, expressed an interest in coming to the colonies. She would wait for them to get settled and send word. Perhaps the most pleased of the entire group was John Parker's mother. Anne's new relation had embraced her new daughter with open arms. She had given her a family brooch and helped with the fitting of Anne's wedding dress. John's father watched the party from the side of the room, puffing his pipe and wishing he were young enough to travel across the sea.

MISS *Moser's Student*

The happy couple were able to book a trip on an East Indian ship bound for the Caribbean with a detour to Philadelphia first. The ocean crossing would take at least six weeks, and soon after their wedding, they worked to pack accordingly. Anne laughed to think of their trunks; only one with clothes and personal items, the other two full of apothecary supplies. John had not compromised on any of it, Anne smiled.

Anne could tell that her own excitement was equaled by her husband's fears. He was afraid of the long journey and worried what concoctions might be necessary for various ailments as they crossed the sea. For every herb he brought to Anne to pack he had a 'what if' story. She had not argued, but she had no such fears herself. Perhaps the difference in their anxiety came from the difference in their upbringing. Anne had suffered several hardships in her years of service, never starvation or dirty accommodations, and those were the only fears she had about the journey.

John's family and Hodges made the small group to see them off. Miss Moser had spoken to Anne earlier. Though the trip to the dock might tax her, it was the sadness of their parting to which the lady deferred. Even as they had said their good-byes that morning, tears were shed on both sides.

"Oh, Anne, words cannot express how happy I am for you. Please know that you are always welcome back at my home. You have become like a daughter to me, and I look forward to hearing of your new life and your efforts towards a new herbal."

Even Millie was blotting tears as Anne talked with her teacher. As Anne hugged the maid for the last time, Miss Moser spoke up.

"Millie will be getting a weekly lesson in the studio." She was proud to tell Anne of the plan as it was Anne who brought the maid's talent to her teacher's attention.

"Oh that is wonderful," Anne replied. So, Miss Moser would have a new student. Perhaps she would not miss Anne as much knowing she had a new purpose.

Now, as the ship was slowly pulling away from the harbor out to where the sails could be set to catch their first wind, Anne's eye overflowed with the tears she had yet to shed. She looked at the shoreline, knowing she might not see her native land for years or perhaps ever again. She left behind a life full of surprises and amazing twists and turns, but as she stood there, wrapped in her husband's arms, she felt ready to take on this new adventure and new skylines in a new world. Safe in her husband's embrace, Anne could not have been prouder. She was the apothecary's wife.

The Captain, Stefan Enman, commanded the ship from the uppermost deck. His haughty voice carried across the entire ship, yelling his orders to the sailors who now scurried about in response.

"Passengers will go below deck," he shouted.

Anne had not liked this man from the first glance she had of him. His features were sharp and his brow furled in the weight of his responsibility. In other circumstances, she might have thought him handsome, but her opinion was prejudiced by his demeanor. He had looked at her with utter disapproval as she entered the ship from the gang plank. His look had hit her as if he held a whip. She had looked away quickly, not sharing his perusal. She hoped as the journey progressed, his attitude toward her would be more tolerant. After all, she had done nothing to raise such ire.

The captain disdained the happy couple who stood looking out toward the bay from which they had just departed. His jealousy came through his voice. The wife was a beauty, he noticed. She would not hold his attention, but he worried she might be a problem as the other sailors would no doubt try to please her. Any challenge to his ultimate control angered him.

"Passengers will go below deck," he repeated. "Now!" He shouted, looking directly at Anne.

The End

www.ingramcontent.com/pod-product-compliance
Lightning Source LLC
Chambersburg PA
CBHW061143040426
42445CB00013B/1527